PRIMARY MATHEMATICS

TEXTBOOK 1B

Common Core Edition

SINGAPORE MATH® PROGRAM

Marshall Cavendish Education

US Distributor

SM Singapore Math Inc.®

W9-BZO-667

BLANK

Original edition published under the title Primary Mathematics Textbook 1B
© 1981 Curriculum Planning & Development Division, Ministry of Education, Singapore
Published by Times Media Private Limited

This edition © 2014 Marshall Cavendish Education Pte Ltd
(Formerly known as Marshall Cavendish International (Singapore) Private Limited)

Published by Marshall Cavendish Education
Times Centre, 1 New Industrial Road, Singapore 536196
Customer Service Hotline: (65) 6213 9444
US Office Tel: (1-914) 332 8888 | Fax: (1-914) 332 8882
E-mail: tmesales@mceducation.com
Website: www.mceducation.com

Distributed by
Singapore Math Inc.®
19535 SW 129th Avenue
Tualatin, OR 97062, U.S.A.
Tel: (503) 557 8100
Website: www.singaporemath.com

First published 2014
Reprinted 2014

Primary Mathematics (Common Core Edition) Textbook 1B
ISBN 978-981-01-9830-5

Printed in Malaysia

Primary Mathematics (Common Core Edition) is adapted from Primary Mathematics Textbook 1B (3rd Edition), originally developed by the Ministry of Education, Singapore. This edition contains new content developed by Marshall Cavendish Education Pte Ltd, which is not attributable to the Ministry of Education, Singapore.

We would like to acknowledge the contributions by:

The Project Team from the Ministry of Education, Singapore, that developed the original Singapore Edition
Project Director: Dr Kho Tek Hong
Team Members: Hector Chee Kum Hoong, Liang Hin Hoon, Lim Eng Tann, Ng Siew Lee, Rosalind Lim Hui Cheng, Ng Hwee Wan

Primary Mathematics (Common Core Edition)
Richard Askey, Emeritus Professor of Mathematics from University of Wisconsin, Madison
Jennifer Kempe, Curriculum Advisor from Singapore Math Inc.®

PREFACE

PRIMARY MATHEMATICS Common Core Edition is a complete program from Marshall Cavendish Education, the publisher of Singapore's successful *Primary Mathematics* series. Newly adapted to align with the Common Core State Standards for mathematics, the program aims to equip students with sound concept development, critical thinking, and efficient problem-solving skills.

Mathematical concepts are introduced in the opening pages and taught to mastery through specific learning tasks that allow for immediate assessment and consolidation.

The **pencil icon**  Exercises 1–2, pages 7–10 provides quick and easy reference from the Textbook to the relevant Workbook pages. The **direct correlation** of the Workbook to the Textbook facilitates focused review and evaluation.

The color patch   is used to invite active student participation and to facilitate lively discussion about the mathematical concepts taught.

The **Concrete → Pictorial → Abstract** approach enables students to encounter math in a meaningful way and translate mathematical skills from the concrete to the abstract.

12

MULTIPLICATION

1 Adding Equal Groups
Count each type of fruit.

40

Fill in the missing number.

$5 + 5 + 5 =$ ☐
3 fives = ☐

There are 5 pears in each group.

$4 + 4 + 4 + 4 + 4 + 4 =$ ☐
6 fours = ☐

There are 4 oranges in each group.

$6 + 6 =$ ☐
2 sixes = ☐

There are 6 pineapples in each group.

41

New mathematical concepts are introduced through a **spiral progression** that builds on concepts already taught and mastered.

4. Add 62 and 30.

$62 + 30 =$ ☐

Count on 3 tens from 62:
72, 82, 92

$62 + 30$
60 2
Add 60 and 30.

Tens	Ones
6	2
+ 3	0

99

Metacognition is employed as a strategy for learners to monitor their thinking processes in problem solving. Speech and thought bubbles provide guidance through the thought processes, making even the most challenging problems accessible to students.

GLOSSARY

Word	Meaning
divide	Tom has **divided** his 6 carrots into 3 equal groups. There are 2 carrots in each group. I'm sharing!
equation	$3 + 3 = 6$ $6 = 3 + 3$ $6 - 3 = 3$ $3 = 6 - 3$ $3 \times 2 = 6$ $6 = 3 \times 2$ These are examples of **equations**.

131

REVIEW 11A

1. 10 more than 28 is _____
   (A) 8
   (B) 18
   (C) 38
   (D) 40

2. $9 + 5 + 6 =$ _____
   (A) 11
   (B) 14
   (C) 15
   (D) 20

...ct True or False.

True / False

There are 15 flowers.

4. Select True or False.
   These numbers are arranged in order, beginning with the smallest:
   15, 25, 35, 33

True / False

36

Regular **reviews** in the Textbook provide consolidation of concept learnt.

The **Glossary** effectively combines pictorial representation with simple mathematical definitions to provide a comprehensive reference guide for students.

CONTENTS

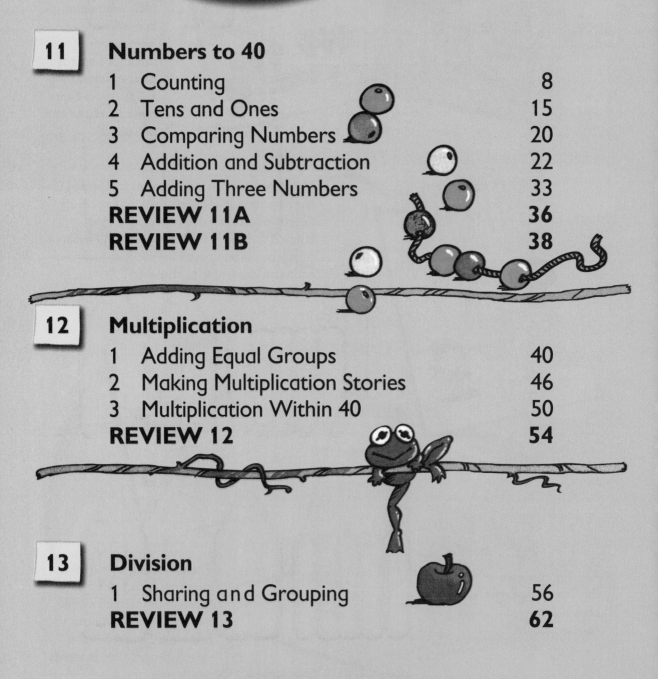

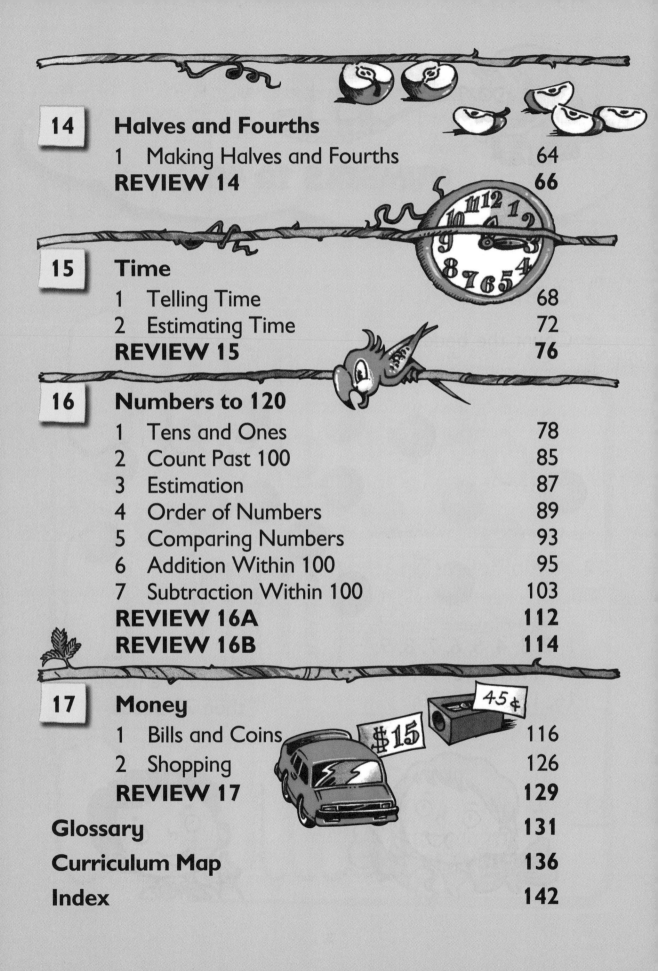

NUMBERS TO 40

1 Counting

Count the beads.

1, 2, 3, 4, 5, 6, 7, 8, 9, 10, 11, 12, 13, 14, 15, 16, 17, 18, 19, 20, . . .

There are more than 20 beads.

Make tens and count.

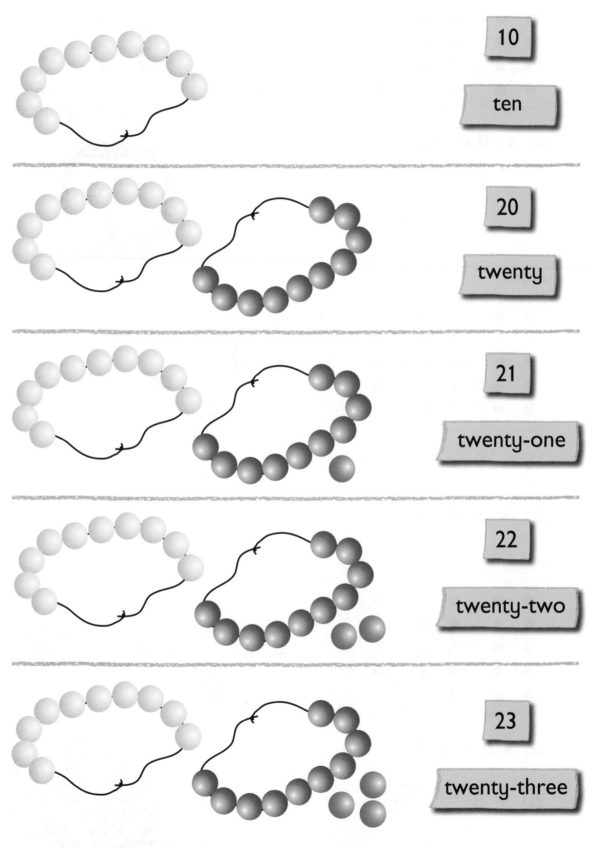

10	ten
20	twenty
21	twenty-one
22	twenty-two
23	twenty-three

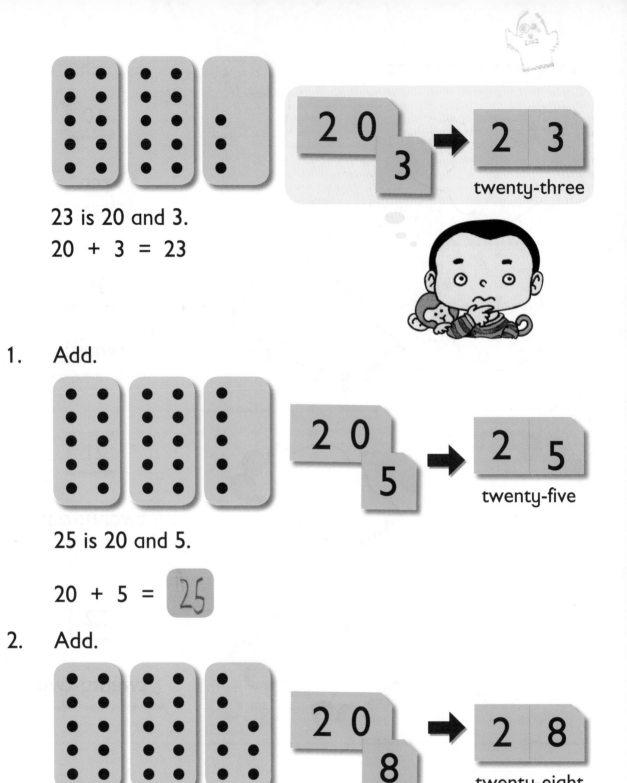

23 is 20 and 3.

$20 + 3 = 23$

twenty-three

1. Add.

25 is 20 and 5.

$20 + 5 = 25$

twenty-five

2. Add.

28 is 20 and 8.

$20 + 8 = 28$

twenty-eight

1	2	3	4	5	6	7	8	9	10
11	12	13	14	15	16	17	18	19	20
21	22	23	24	25	26	27	28	29	30
31	32	33	34	35	36	37	38	39	40

3. Add.

29 and 1 make 30.

29 + 1 = 30

10, 20, 30

3 0

thirty

4. Add.

30 0 → 3 4
4

thirty-four

30 and 4 make 34.

30 + 4 = 34

11

5. Add.

4 0

forty

1 more than 39 is 40.

39 + 1 = 40

Exercises 1–2, pages 7–10

6. (a) How many sticks are there?

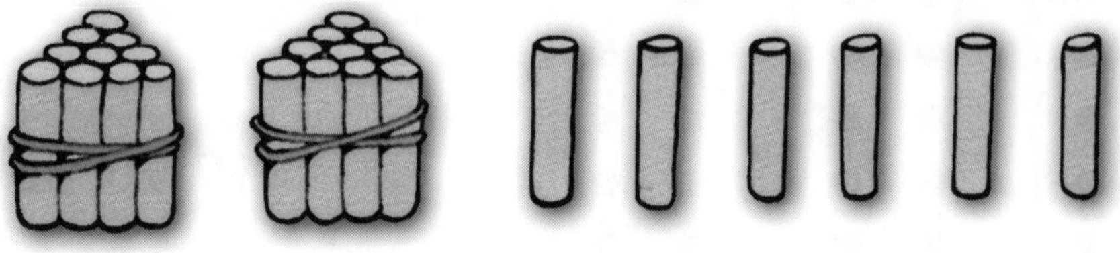

(b) 20 + 6 = 26

(c) 6 more than 20 is 26.

7. (a) How many strawberries are there?

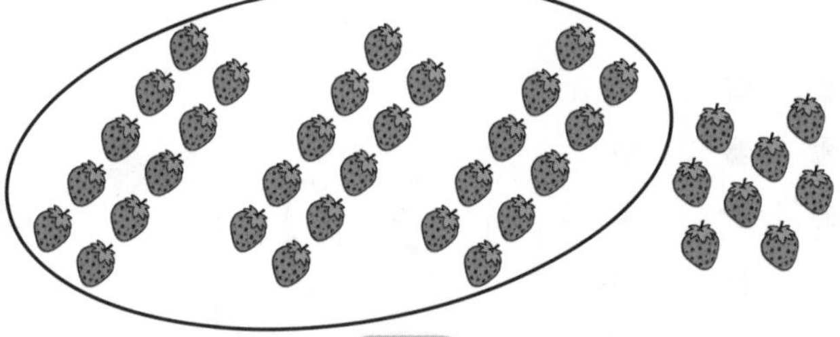

(b) 30 + 8 = 38

(c) 8 more than 30 is 38.

Exercise 3, page 11

8. Complete the equations.

(a)

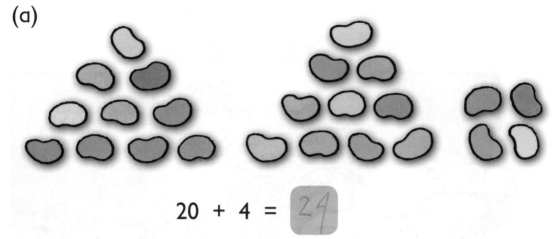

20 + 4 = 24

(b)

20 + 7 = 27

(c)

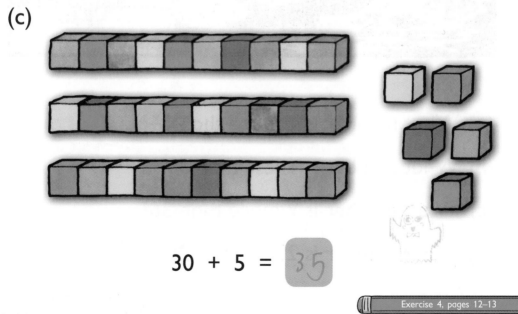

30 + 5 = 35

Exercise 4, pages 12–13

9. What are the missing numbers?

18, 19, 20, 21, 22, . . .

10. (a) What number is 1 more than 24?

(b) What number is 1 less than 30?

(c) What number is 2 more than 36?

(d) What number is 2 less than 28?

Exercise 5, pages 14–15

2 Tens and Ones

There are 3 tens and 4 loose ones.

10 ones = 1 ten

30 ones = 3 tens

Tens	Ones
3	4

34 = 3 tens 4 ones

3 0
4

thirty-four

1. Write the missing numbers.

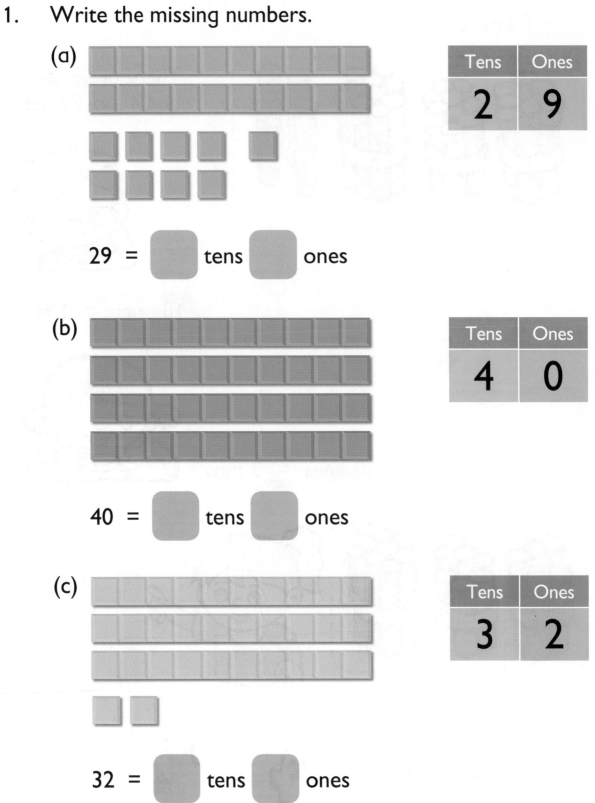

(a)

Tens	Ones
2	9

29 = ☐ tens ☐ ones

(b)

Tens	Ones
4	0

40 = ☐ tens ☐ ones

(c)

Tens	Ones
3	2

32 = ☐ tens ☐ ones

2. Write the missing numbers.

(a)

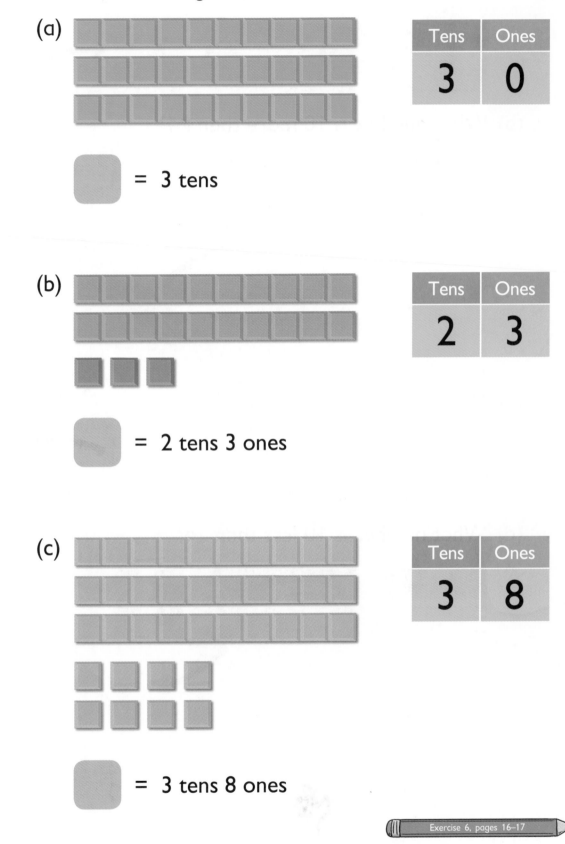

Tens	Ones
3	0

☐ = 3 tens

(b)

Tens	Ones
2	3

☐ = 2 tens 3 ones

(c)

Tens	Ones
3	8

☐ = 3 tens 8 ones

Exercise 6, pages 16–17

3. (a) What number is 1 more than 24?

(b) What number is 10 more than 24?

(c) What number is 1 less than 24?

(d) What number is 10 less than 24?

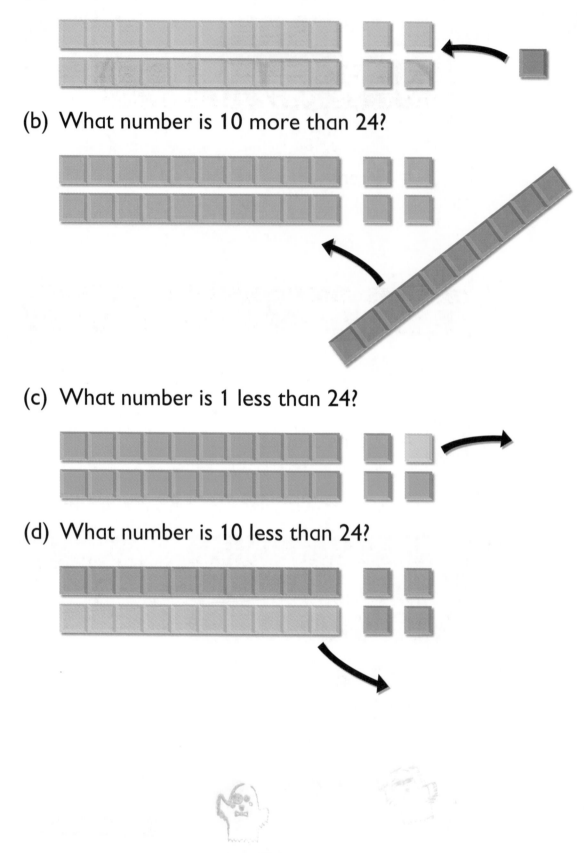

4. (a) What number is 1 more than 29?

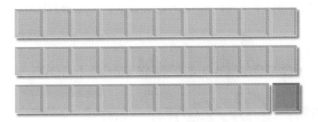

(b) What number is 1 less than 40?

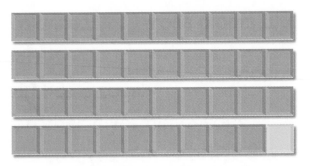

(c) What number is 10 more than 30?

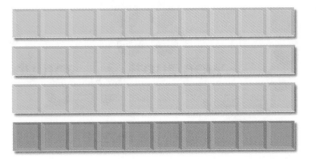

(d) What number is 10 less than 30?

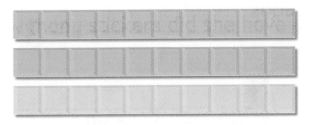

Exercise 7, pages 18–20

③ Comparing Numbers

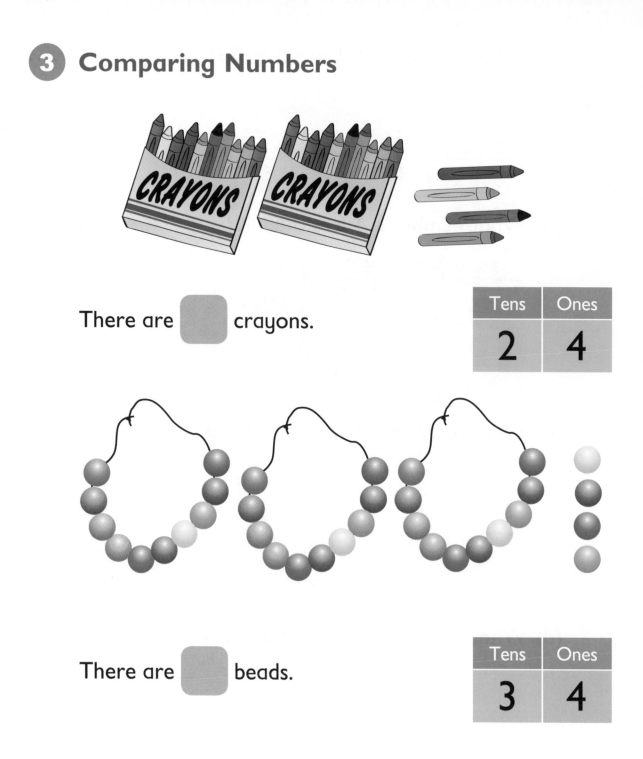

There are ⬜ crayons.

Tens	Ones
2	4

There are ⬜ beads.

Tens	Ones
3	4

Are there more crayons or more beads?

1. (a) Which is greater, 24 or 27?

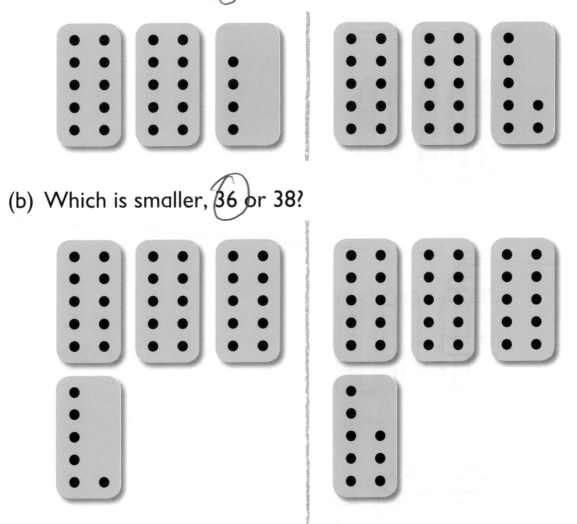

(b) Which is smaller, 36 or 38?

2. (a) Which is greater, 22 or 30?
   (b) Which is smaller, 23 or 39?

3. Compare these numbers.

   (a) Which number is the greatest?

   (b) Which number is the smallest?

   (c) Arrange the numbers in order.
       Begin with the smallest.

34   14

37   24

Exercise 8, page 21

4 Addition and Subtraction

Add or subtract.

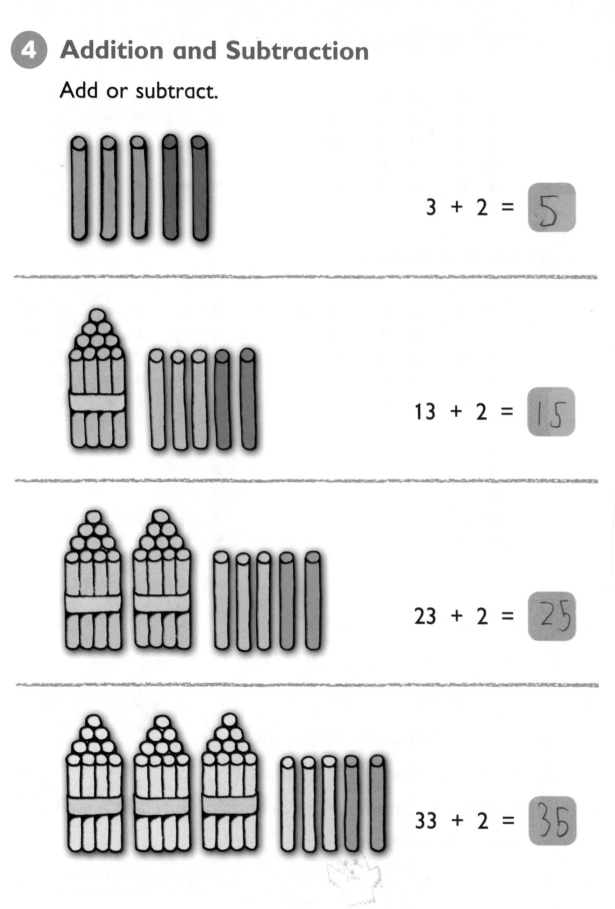

3 + 2 = 5

13 + 2 = 15

23 + 2 = 25

33 + 2 = 35

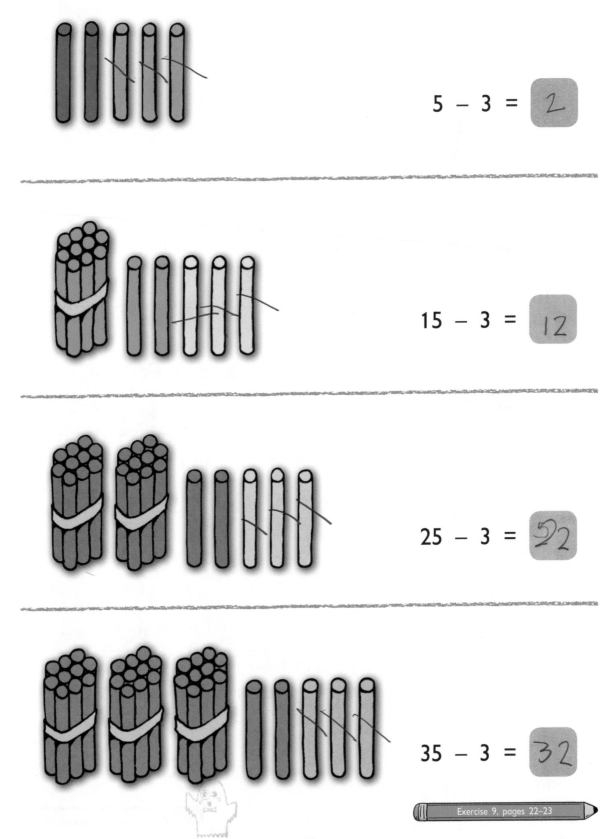

$5 - 3 = \boxed{2}$

$15 - 3 = \boxed{12}$

$25 - 3 = \boxed{22}$

$35 - 3 = \boxed{32}$

Exercise 9, pages 22–23

1. Add and subtract.

(a)

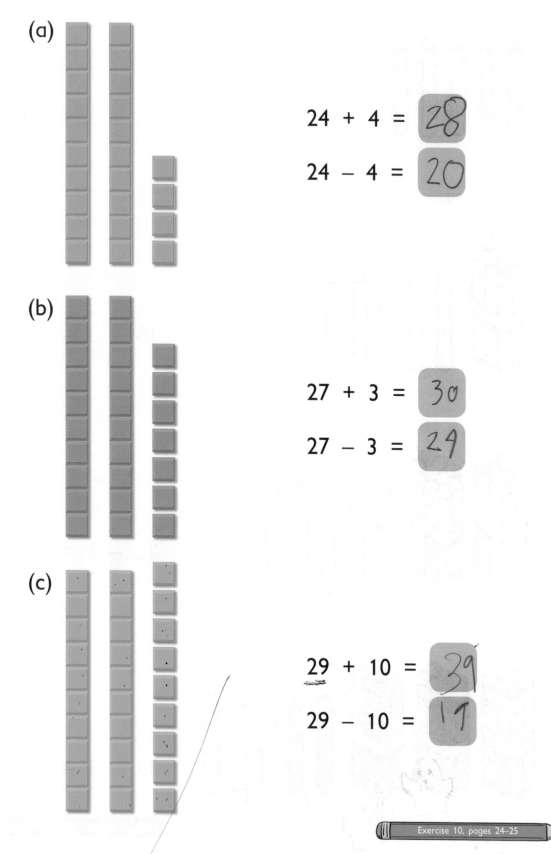

$24 + 4 =$ 28

$24 - 4 =$ 20

(b)

$27 + 3 =$ 30

$27 - 3 =$ 24

(c)

$29 + 10 =$ 39

$29 - 10 =$ 19

Exercise 10, pages 24–25

2. Add 29 and 3.

Count on from 29:
30, 31, 32

29 + 3 = 32

3. Subtract 2 from 31.

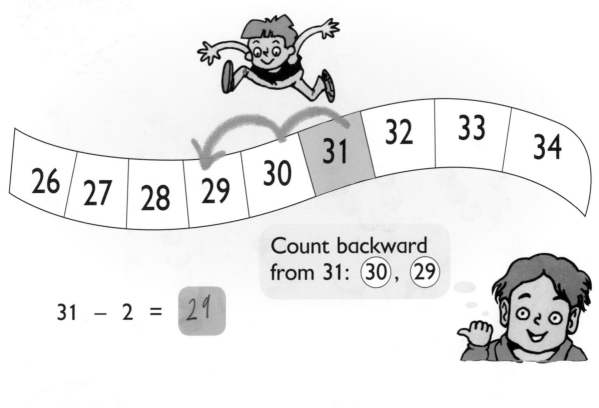

Count backward from 31: 30, 29

31 – 2 = 29

Exercise 11, pages 26–27

4. Add.

(a)

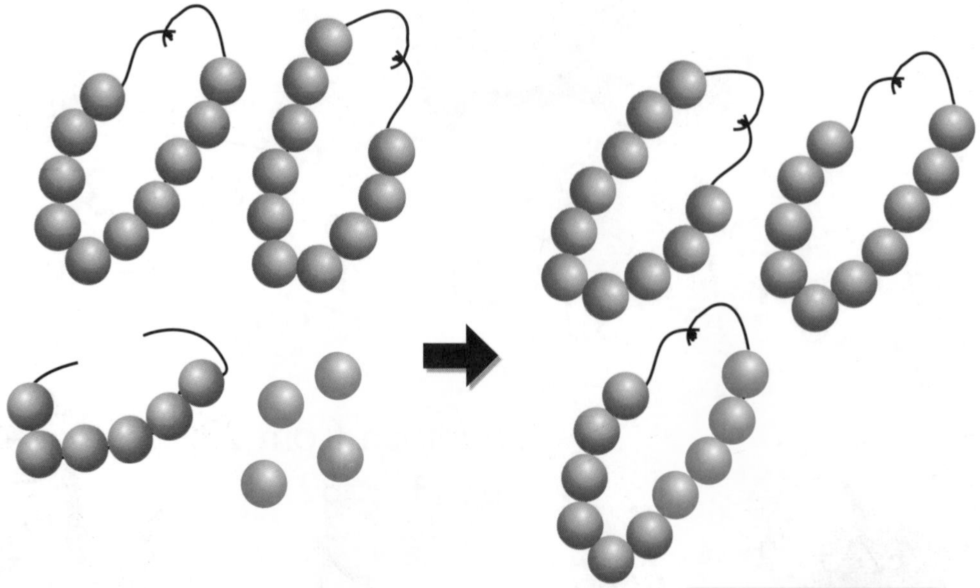

$26 + 4 = \boxed{30}$

$6 + 4 = 10$

(b)

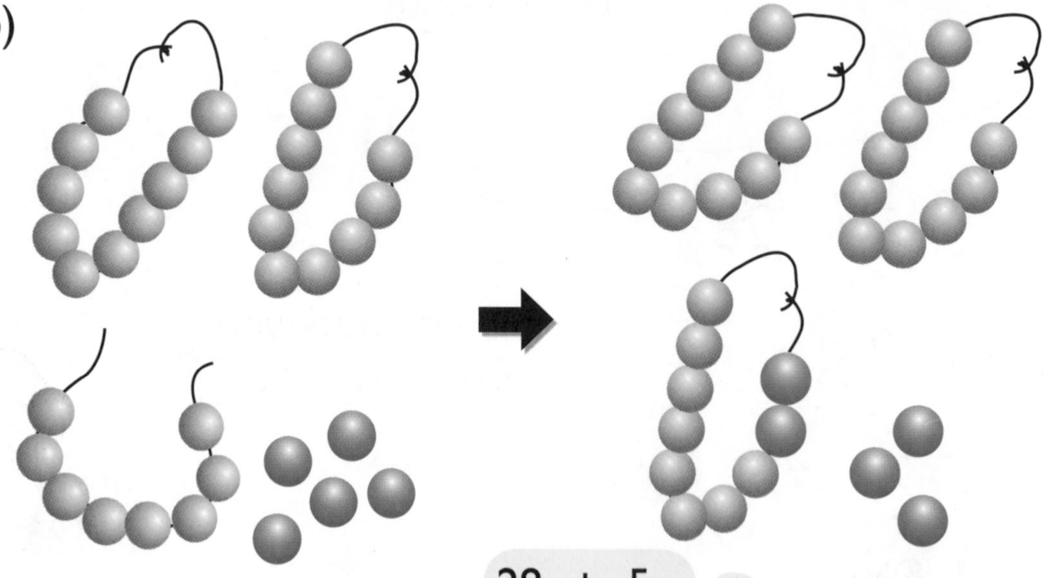

$28 + 5 = \boxed{33}$

$28 + \underset{2 \quad 3}{5}$

26

5. Add.

(a)

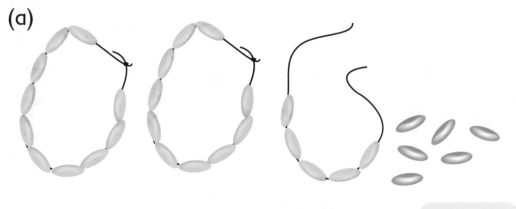

$$25 + 6 = \boxed{31}$$

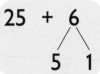

25 + 6
  ⁄ \
 5   1

(b)

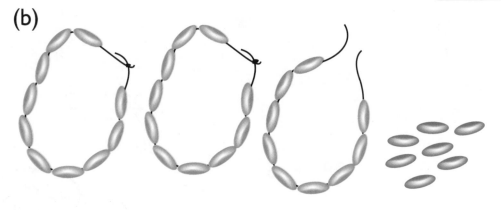

$$29 + 7 = \boxed{36}$$

(c)

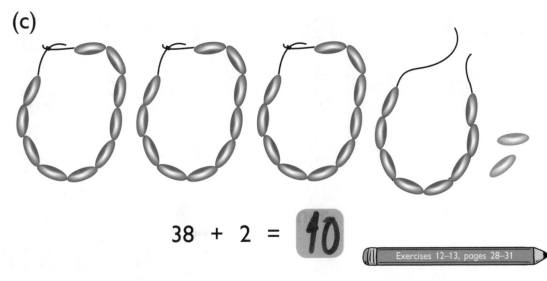

$$38 + 2 = \boxed{40}$$

Exercises 12–13, pages 28–31

6. Add.

(a)

$$8 + 5 = \boxed{}$$

(b)

$$28 + 5$$
$$\diagup \quad \diagdown$$
$$20 \quad 8$$

$$28 + 5 = \boxed{}$$

7. Complete the addition equations.

(a) $9 + 6 = \boxed{}$

$\quad\;\; 19 + 6 = \boxed{}$

(b) $3 + 9 = \boxed{}$

$\quad\;\; 23 + 9 = \boxed{}$

(c) $5 + 7 = \boxed{}$

$\quad\;\; 25 + 7 = \boxed{}$

(d) $3 + 7 = \boxed{}$

$\quad\;\; 33 + 7 = \boxed{}$

Exercises 14–15, pages 32–34

8. Complete the subtraction equation.

(a)

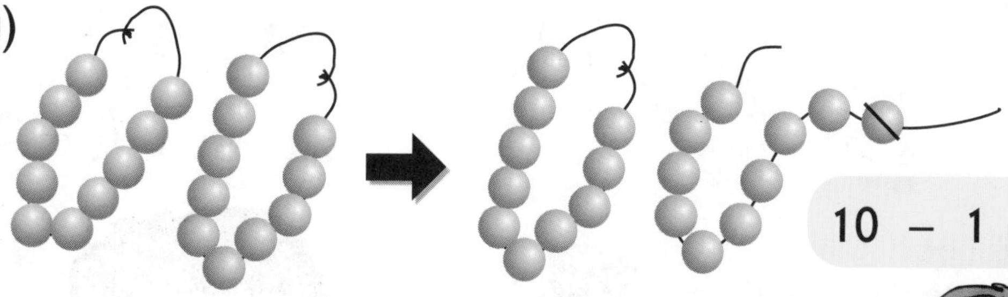

$$10 - 1 = 9$$

$$20 - 1 = \boxed{19}$$

(b)

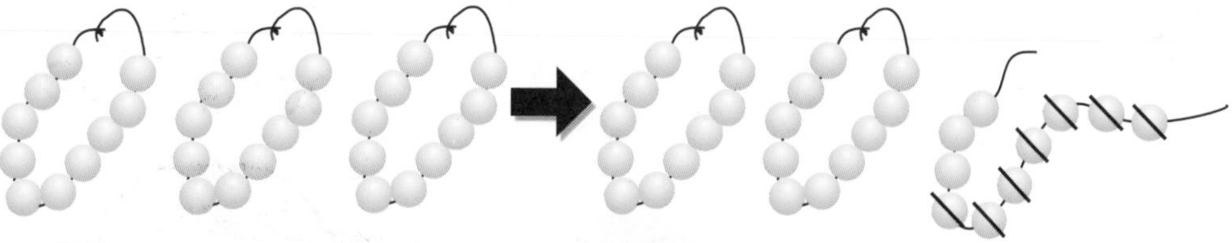

$$30 - 7 = \boxed{23}$$

(c)

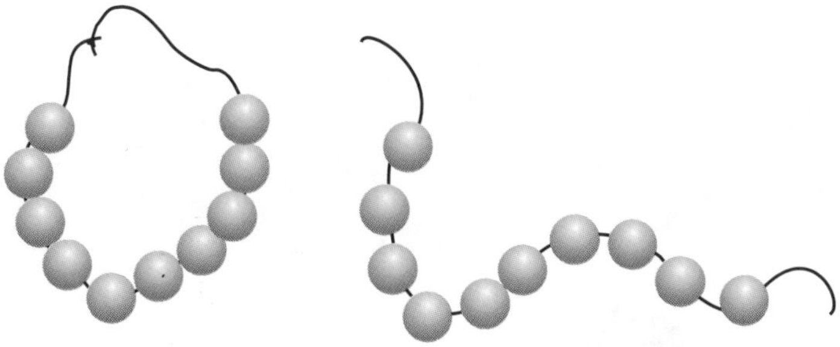

$$20 - 6 = \boxed{14}$$

(d)

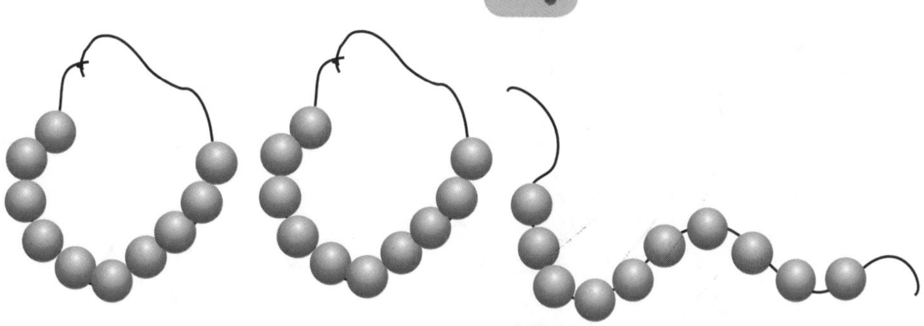

$$30 - 8 = \boxed{22}$$

Exercise 16, pages 35–36

9. Complete the subtraction equations.

(a)

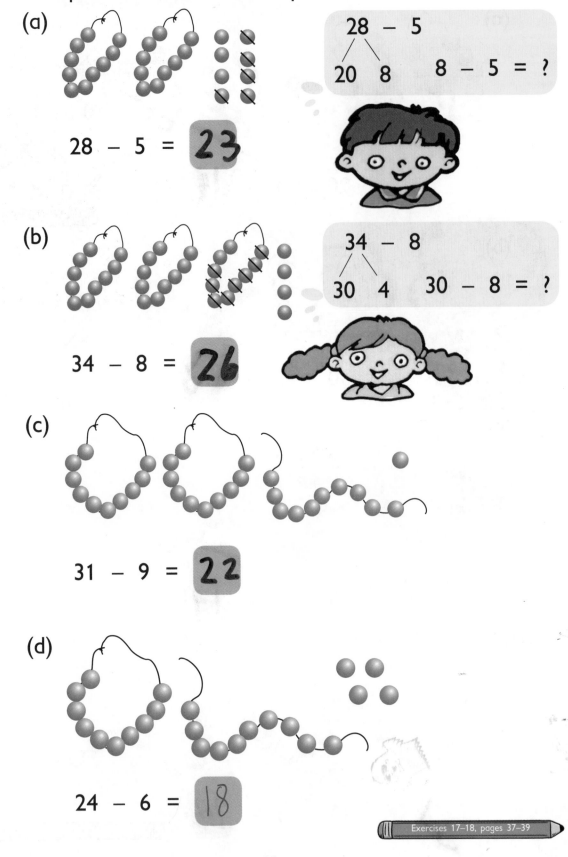

28 − 5

20   8   8 − 5 = ?

28 − 5 = 23

(b)

34 − 8

30   4   30 − 8 = ?

34 − 8 = 26

(c)

31 − 9 = 22

(d)

24 − 6 = 18

Exercises 17–18, pages 37–39

10. Complete the subtraction equations.

(a)

13 − 7

        / \
       3   4

13 − 3 = 10
10 − 4 = ?

13 − 7 = 6

(b)

33 − 7

    / \
   20 13

13 − 7 = ?

33 − 7 = 16

11. Complete the subtraction equations.

(a) 19 − 6 = 13

    29 − 6 = 23

(b) 13 − 9 = 6

    33 − 9 = 24

(c) 15 − 7 = 8

    25 − 7 = 18

(d) 11 − 5 = 6

    31 − 5 = 26

12. Dan baked 14 apple pies and 7 cherry pies.
How many pies did Dan bake altogether?

14 + 7 = 23

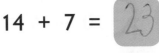

Dan baked 23 pies altogether.

13. Seth drew 23 cars in the morning.
He drew 9 cars in the afternoon.
How many cars did Seth draw altogether?

Seth drew [ ] balloons altogether.

14. Ashley had some stamps.
Her father gave her 6 stamps.
She then had 35 stamps altogether.
How many stamps did Ashley have at first?

Ashley had [ ] stamps at first.

15. Kim bought 38 roses.
She gave her mother 8 roses.
How many roses did Kim have left?

Kim had [ ] roses left.

Exercise 19, pages 40–42

5 Adding Three Numbers

Add.

$8 + 2 = \boxed{10}$

$8 + 2 + 4 = \boxed{14}$

1. Complete the addition equations.

(a)

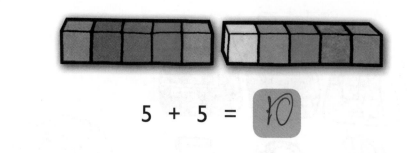

$$5 + 5 = \boxed{10}$$

(b)

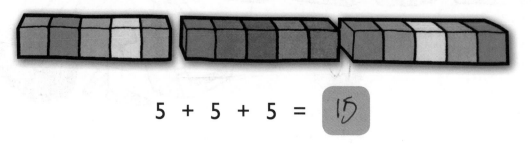

$$5 + 5 + 5 = \boxed{15}$$

2. Complete the addition equations.

(a) $4 + 4 + 4 = \boxed{12}$ (b) $6 + 4 + 3 = \boxed{13}$

(c) $3 + 2 + 9 = \boxed{14}$ (d) $6 + 6 + 6 = \boxed{18}$

(e) $7 + 5 + 4 = \boxed{16}$ (f) $8 + 6 + 2 = \boxed{16}$

(g) $8 + 7 + 3 = \boxed{20}$ (h) $8 + 8 + 8 = \boxed{24}$

Exercise 20, pages 43–45

3. Ken planted 4 rose plants on Monday.
He planted 7 rose plants on Tuesday and 2 rose plants on Wednesday.
How many rose plants did Ken plant altogether?

4 + 7 + 2 = 13

Ken planted 13 rose plants altogether.

4. Randy has 5 toys.
His brother gives him 5 toys.
His sister gives him another 8 toys.
How many toys does Randy have now?

Randy has ⬜ toys now.

5. Emma had some stickers.
She gave 6 stickers to Alan and 9 stickers to David.
She had 4 stickers left.
How many stickers did she have at first?

Emma had ⬜ stickers at first.

Exercise 21, pages 46–47

1. 10 more than 28 is _____.

   (A) 8
   (B) 18
   (C) 38
   (D) 40

2. 9 + 5 + 6 = _____

   (A) 11
   (B) 14
   (C) 15
   (D) 20

3. Select True or False.

   There are 15 flowers.   True / False

4. Select True or False.
   These numbers are arranged in order, beginning with
   the smallest:
   15, 25, 35, 33   True / False

5. Add or subtract.

   (a) 19 + 5   (b) 27 + 3

   (c) 26 + 6   (d) 5 + 28

   (e) 30 − 8   (f) 29 − 4

   (g) 40 − 3   (h) 22 − 6

   (i) 3 + 8 + 7   (j) 9 + 4 + 6

6. Eva played a hopping game.
   She hopped 6 spaces, then another 8 spaces,
   and then another 4 spaces.
   How many spaces did she hop altogether?

7. 23 people are at a swimming pool.
   8 more people come to the pool.
   How many people are at the pool now?

8. Sue has 22 pears.
   Mary has 20 pears.
   Sue gives away 5 pears.
   Mary gives away 2 pears.
   Who has fewer pears now?
   Explain your answer.

1. 3 more than 37 is _____.

   (A) 17

   (B) 30

   (C) 34

   (D) 40

2. 8 + 6 + 7 = _____

   (A) 13

   (B) 15

   (C) 20

   (D) 21

3. Select True or False.

   2 and 28 make 30.   True / False

4. Select True or False.

   There are 15 books.   True / False

5. Add or subtract.

   (a) 18 + 6   (b) 29 + 4

   (c) 3 + 19   (d) 9 + 31

   (e) 30 − 6   (f) 28 − 7

   (g) 40 − 8   (h) 39 − 1

   (i) 4 + 9 + 7   (j) 3 + 10 + 5

6. There are 40 children in the library.
   9 of them wear glasses.
   How many children do not wear glasses?

7. Joseph baked some muffins.
   He then gave 5 muffins to his father, 4 muffins to his
   mother, and 3 muffins to his sister.
   He had no muffins left.
   How many muffins did Joseph bake?

8. Gina has 28 marbles.
   Eva has 34 marbles.
   Gina buys 4 more marbles.
   Eva gives away 2 marbles.
   Who has more marbles now?
   Explain your answer.

Workbook Review 11, pages 48–52

12 MULTIPLICATION

1 Adding Equal Groups

Count each type of fruit.

Fill in the missing number.

$5 + 5 + 5 =$ 15

3 fives $=$ 15

There are 5 pears in each group.

9 8 12 16 20 21

$4 + 4 + 4 + 4 + 4 + 4 =$ 21

6 fours $=$

There are 4 oranges in each group.

$6 + 6 =$ 12

2 sixes $=$

There are 6 pineapples in each group.

Fill in the missing number.

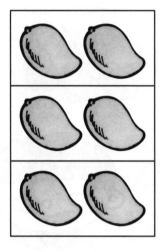

$2 + 2 + 2 =$

3 twos $=$

There are 2 mangoes in each row.

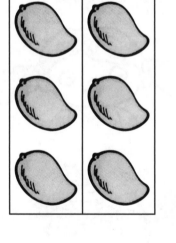

$3 + 3 =$

2 threes $=$

There are 3 mangoes in each column.

Write the missing numbers.

1.

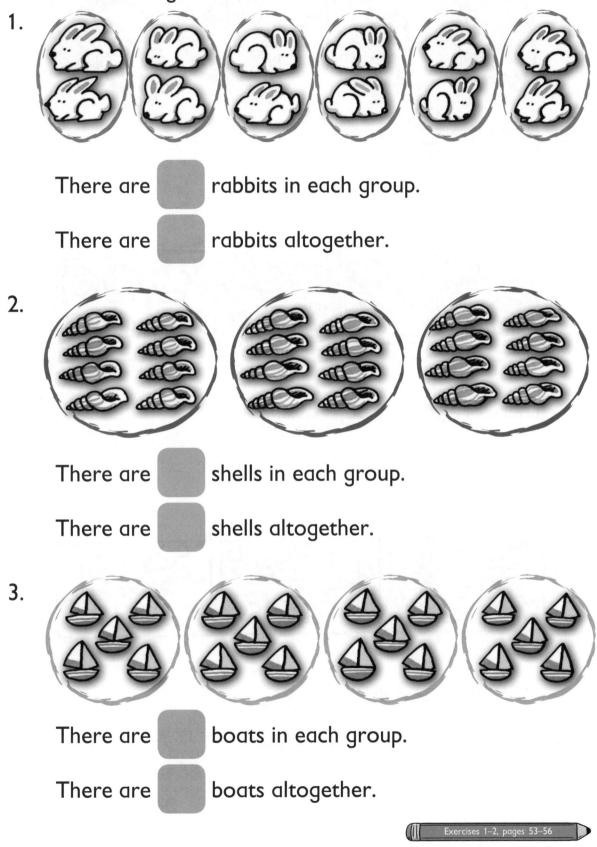

There are ▢ rabbits in each group.

There are ▢ rabbits altogether.

2.

There are ▢ shells in each group.

There are ▢ shells altogether.

3.

There are ▢ boats in each group.

There are ▢ boats altogether.

Exercises 1–2, pages 53–56

4.

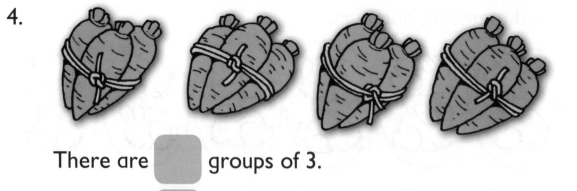

There are ☐ groups of 3.

There are ☐ carrots altogether.

5.

There are ☐ groups of 4.

There are ☐ cupcakes altogether.

6.

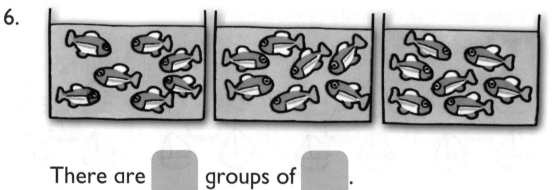

There are 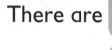 groups of  .

There are ☐ fish altogether.

7.

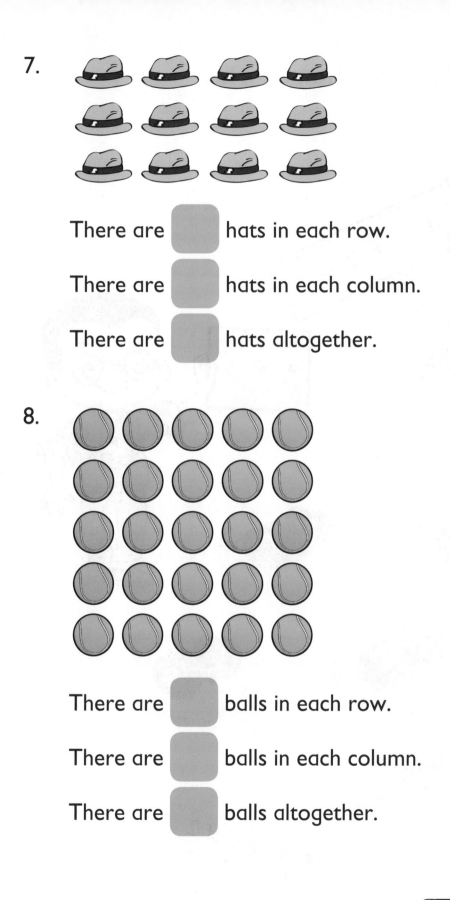

There are ⬜ hats in each row.

There are ⬜ hats in each column.

There are ⬜ hats altogether.

8.

There are ⬜ balls in each row.

There are ⬜ balls in each column.

There are ⬜ balls altogether.

Exercise 3, pages 57–59

This is **multiplication**. It means **putting together equal groups**.

We write the multiplication equation:

$$4 \times 2 = 8$$

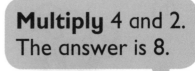

Multiply 4 and 2. The answer is 8.

There are 4 equal groups.
There are 2 apples in each group.
There are 8 apples altogether.
4 times 2 **equals** 8.

1. Make up a story for each multiplication equation.

(a)

$$4 \times 3 = 12$$

There are 4 vases.
There are 3 flowers in each vase.
There are 12 flowers altogether.

(b)

$$4 \times 5 = 20$$

(c)

$$4 \times 8 = 32$$

2. Make up a story for each multiplication equation.

(a)

$$4 \times 6 = 24$$

(b)

$$6 \times 4 = 24$$

Exercises 4–5, pages 60–62

3 Multiplication Within 40

Multiply.

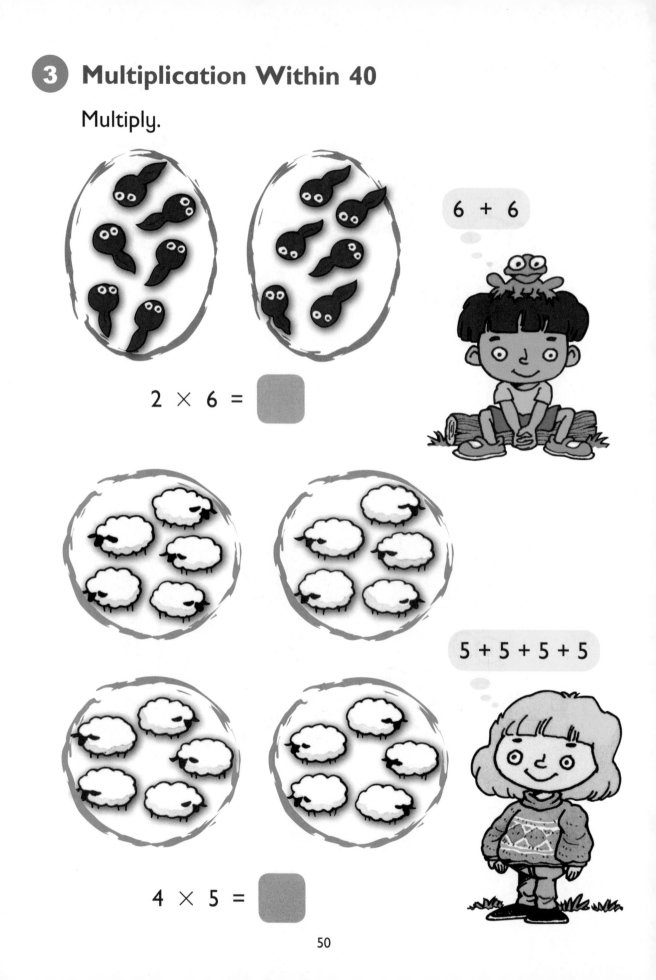

6 + 6

2 × 6 = ☐

5 + 5 + 5 + 5

4 × 5 = ☐

50

1.

How many pears are there altogether?

$$3 \times 2 = \boxed{}$$

There are $\boxed{}$ pears altogether.

2.

How many sticks are there altogether?

$$4 \times 5 = \boxed{}$$

There are $\boxed{}$ sticks altogether.

3. Complete the multiplication equations.

(a)

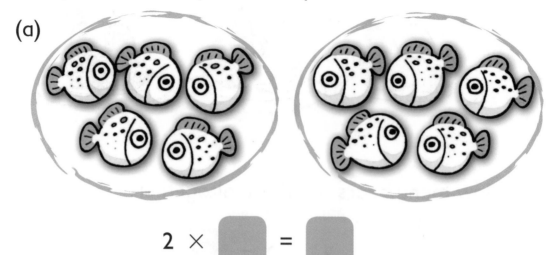

$$2 \times \boxed{} = \boxed{}$$

(b)

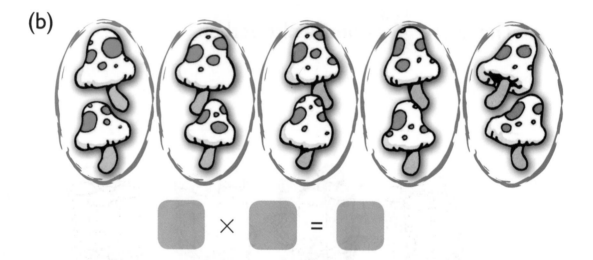

$$\boxed{} \times \boxed{} = \boxed{}$$

(c)

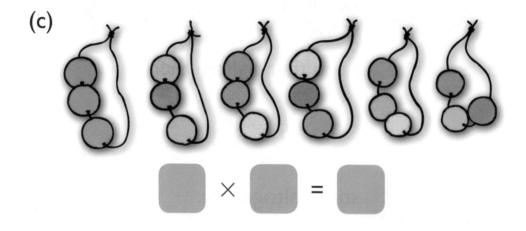

$$\boxed{} \times \boxed{} = \boxed{}$$

Exercise 6, pages 63–65

4.

There are 6 stamps in each row.
How many stamps are there in 3 rows?

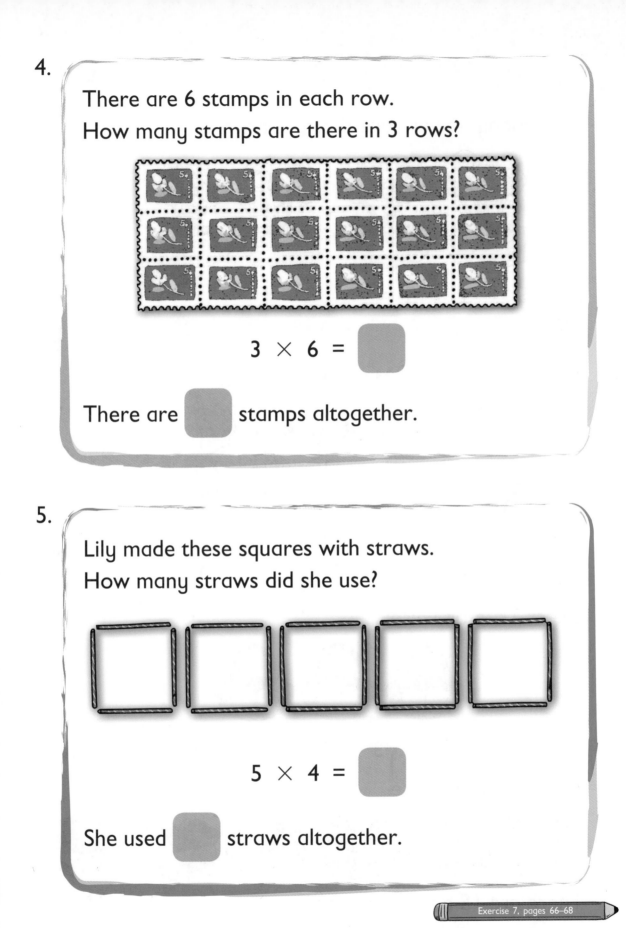

$3 \times 6 = $ ▢

There are ▢ stamps altogether.

5.

Lily made these squares with straws.
How many straws did she use?

$5 \times 4 = $ ▢

She used ▢ straws altogether.

Exercise 7, pages 66–68

1. How many flowers are there altogether?

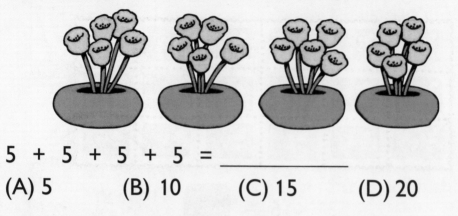

5 + 5 + 5 + 5 = _____

(A) 5   (B) 10   (C) 15   (D) 20

2. How many butterflies are there altogether?

There are _____ butterflies altogether.

(A) 4   (B) 8   (C) 12   (D) 15

3. Select True or False.

$$3 \times 2 = 6$$ True / False

4. Select True or False.

There are 15 balls altogether.   True / False

5. Write a multiplication equation for this picture.

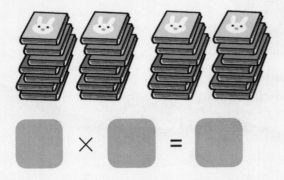

◻ × ◻ = ◻

6. An elephant has 4 legs.

How many legs do 6 elephants have?

7.

How many glasses are there altogether?

Susan wrote: 5 + 5 + 5 = 15

Philip wrote: 3 + 3 + 3 + 3 + 3 = 15

Whose addition equation correctly describes the picture above? Explain your answer.

Workbook Review 12, pages 69–71

13 DIVISION

1 Sharing and Grouping

I put 15 apples equally on 3 plates.

Divide 15 apples into 3 equal groups.

There are ☐ apples in each group.

I put 3 apples in a group.

Divide 15 apples into groups of 3.

There are ☐ groups.

1. Divide 10 children into 2 equal groups.
   How many children are there in each group?

There are ☐ children in each group.

2. Share 12 kiwis equally between 2 children.
   How many kiwis does each child get?

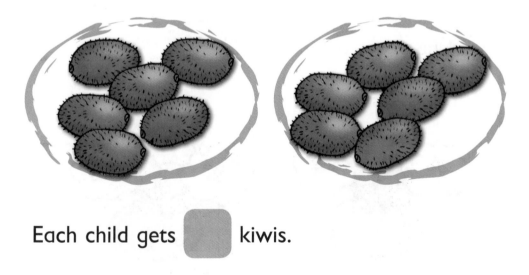

Each child gets ☐ kiwis.

3.   Put 14 crayons equally into 2 boxes.
     How many crayons are there in each box?

There are  crayons in each box.

Exercise 1, pages 72–75

4.   There are 6 flowers.
     Put 3 flowers in a vase.
     How many vases are needed?

vases are needed.

5. There are 20 coins.
   Put 5 coins in a group.
   How many groups are there?

There are ☐ groups.

6. Divide 12 mangoes into groups of 3.
   How many groups are there?

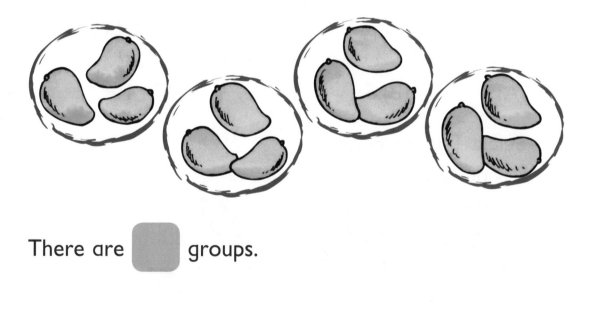

There are ☐ groups.

Exercises 2–3, pages 76–79

1.

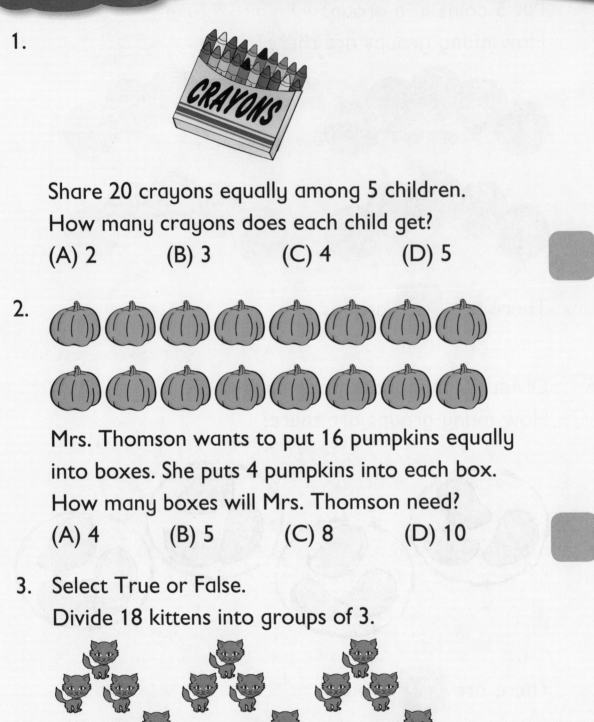

Share 20 crayons equally among 5 children.
How many crayons does each child get?
(A) 2   (B) 3   (C) 4   (D) 5

2.

Mrs. Thomson wants to put 16 pumpkins equally
into boxes. She puts 4 pumpkins into each box.
How many boxes will Mrs. Thomson need?
(A) 4   (B) 5   (C) 8   (D) 10

3. Select True or False.
   Divide 18 kittens into groups of 3.

There are 6 groups.   True / False

4. Select True or False.

Gillian puts 25 pencils equally into 5 boxes.

There are 5 pencils in each box.   True / False

5.

(a) How many pieces of candy are there?

(b) Mary wants to divide the candy into baskets so that there are 6 pieces in each basket.

How many baskets does she need?

(c) Mary only has 3 baskets.

She divides the candy equally into the 3 baskets.

How many pieces of candy are in each basket?

6. Simon wants to divide 8 muffins equally between David and John.

He gives 5 muffins to David and 3 muffins to John.

Is Simon correct? Explain your answer.

Workbook Review 13, pages 80–83

HALVES AND FOURTHS

1 Making Halves and Fourths

Fold a piece of square paper into **halves**.

Then fold it into **fourths** or **quarters**.

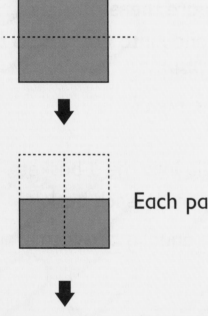

Each part is one half.

Each part is one fourth, or one quarter.

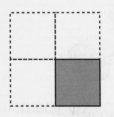

Think of other ways to fold the paper into halves and fourths.

1. Which is smaller, a half of the orange or a fourth of the orange?

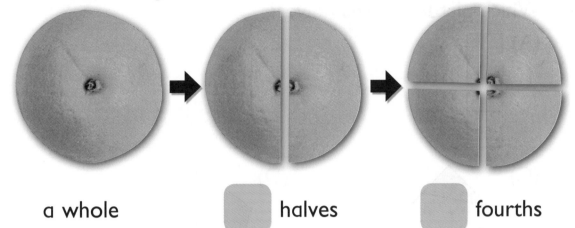

a whole   halves   fourths

2. Which pictures show halves?

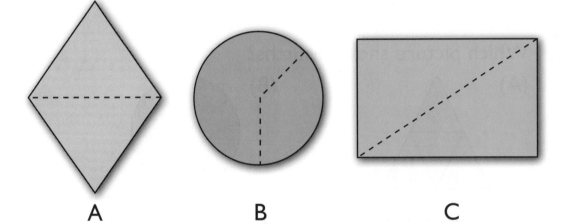

A   B   C

3. Which pictures show quarters?

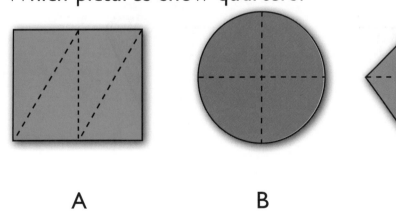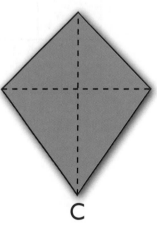

A   B   C

Exercises 1–2, pages 84–87

1. Which picture shows halves?

(A)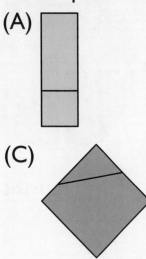

(B)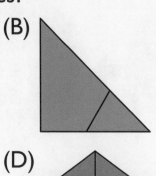

(C)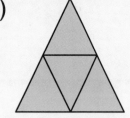

(D)

2. Which picture shows fourths?

(A)

(B)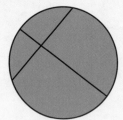

(C)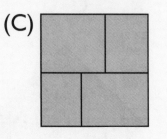

(D)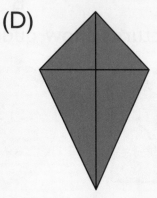

3. Select True or False.

The picture shows quarters.   True / False

4. Select True or False.

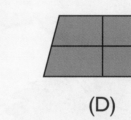

The picture shows halves.   True / False

5. Which pictures show fourths?

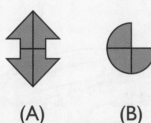 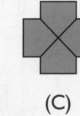

(A)   (B)   (C)   (D)

6. Sue cuts a piece of square paper into quarters.

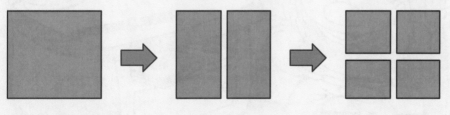

Is each piece a quarter of the square paper?
Explain your answer.

Workbook Review 14, pages 88–90

15 TIME

1 Telling Time

It is 6 **o'clock** in the morning.

1. **What time is it?**

Exercise 1, pages 91–93

2.   What time is it?

It is 4 o'clock.

It is four thirty.

It is ⬜ o'clock.

It is ⬜ thirty.

It is **half past** ⬜.

3. What time is it?

Exercise 2, pages 94–96

2 Estimating Time

It is after 9 o'clock.

It is not 10 o'clock yet.

It is close to 10 o'clock.

It is a **little before** 10 o'clock.

It is **about** 10 o'clock.

It is after 1 o'clock.

It is not half past 1 yet.

It is **almost** half past 1.

It is about one thirty.

It is after 11 o'clock.

It is a **little after** 11 o'clock.

It is about 11 o'clock.

1. Mr. Smith gets up after 7 o'clock.

(a) Does he have breakfast **before** 9:00?

(b) Does he leave for work **after** half past 7?

2. Estimate the time.

(a) 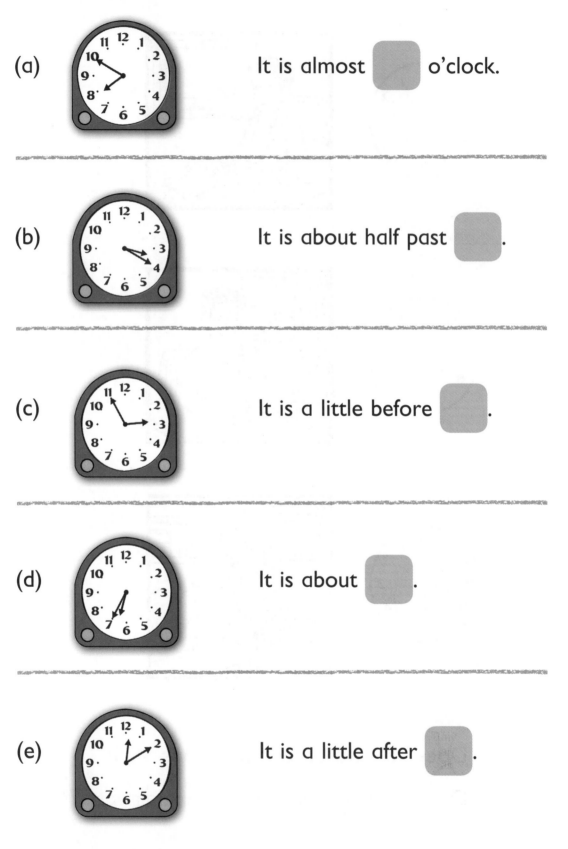 It is almost ▢ o'clock.

(b) It is about half past ▢.

(c) It is a little before ▢.

(d) It is about ▢.

(e) It is a little after ▢.

3. Which takes longer?

(a)  or

(b)  or

(c)  or

Exercise 3, pages 97–98

1.

   It is _____.

   (A) 8 o'clock   (B) half past 8

   (C) 9 o'clock   (D) half past 9

2. Mrs. Johnson went to the supermarket at half past 7.

   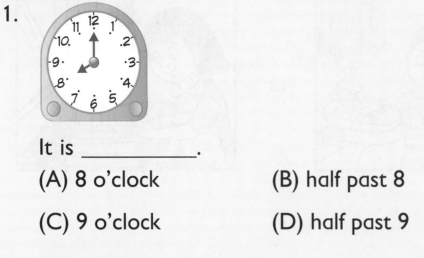

   The missing number in the clock is _____.

   (A) 20   (B) 30   (C) 40   (D) 50

The pictures show what David does at different times.
Use the pictures to answer questions 3 to 5.

3. Select True or False.
   David bathes before 5 o'clock.   True / False

4. Select True or False.
   David has dinner at half past 7.   True / False

5. Select True or False.
   David reads a book after half past 6.   True / False

6. What time is it?

   (a)    (b)   (c)

7. About what time is it?

   (a)   (b)   (c)

8.

   Are the two clocks showing the same time?
   Explain your answer.

Workbook Review 15, pages 99–103

16 NUMBERS TO 120

1 Tens and Ones

Count by tens.   10, … 20, … 30, … 40

Count.

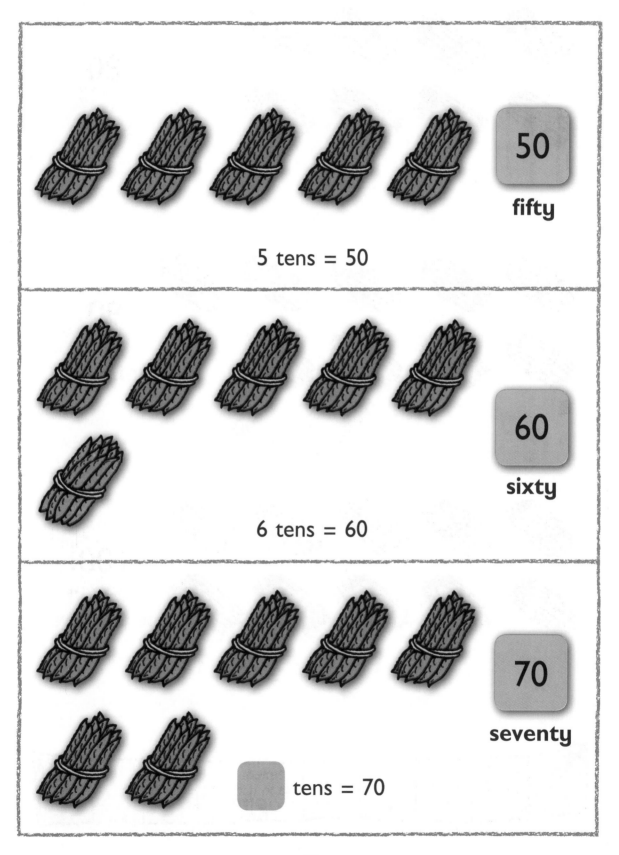

50
fifty

5 tens = 50

60
sixty

6 tens = 60

70
seventy

tens = 70

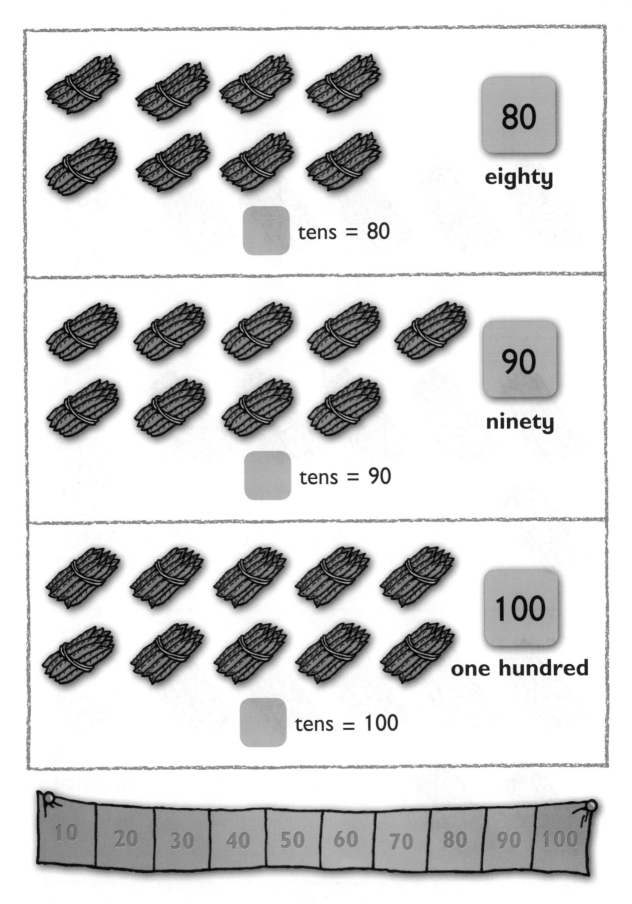

80

eighty

tens = 80

90

ninety

tens = 90

100

one hundred

tens = 100

| 10 | 20 | 30 | 40 | 50 | 60 | 70 | 80 | 90 | 100 |

1. Count.

(a)

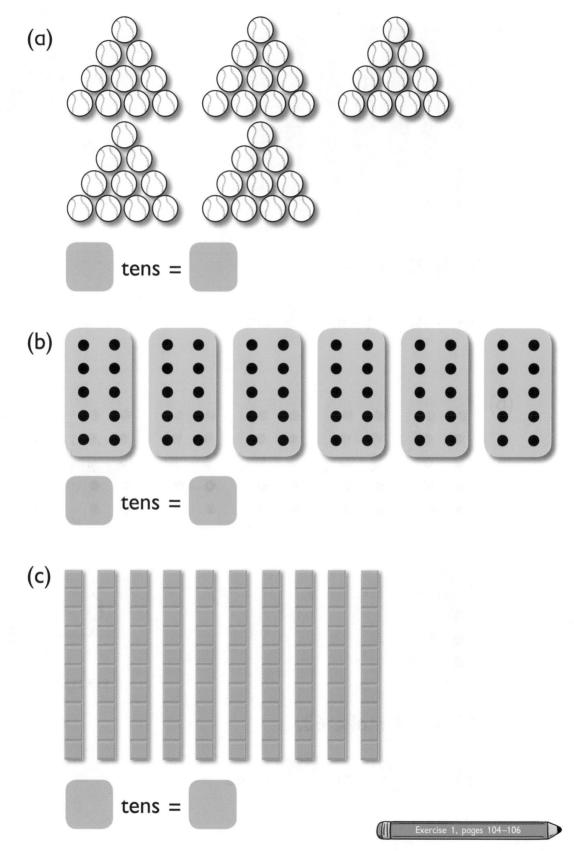

[   ]   tens = [   ]

(b)

[   ]   tens = [   ]

(c)

[   ]   tens = [   ]

Exercise 1, pages 104–106

2. Fill in the missing numbers.

(a)

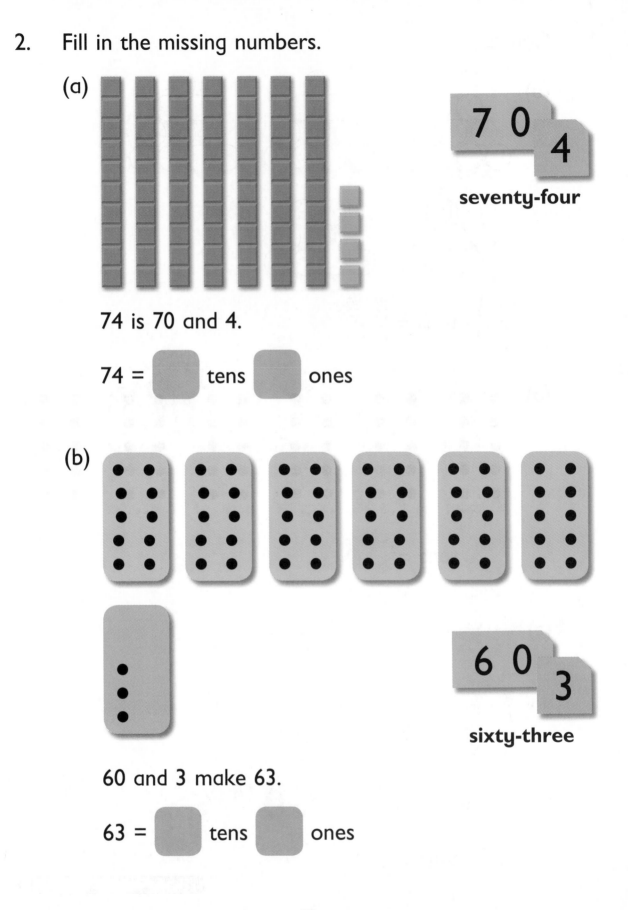

7 0 4

seventy-four

74 is 70 and 4.

74 = ⬜ tens ⬜ ones

(b)

60 and 3 make 63.

6 0 3

sixty-three

63 = ⬜ tens ⬜ ones

3. Count.

(a)

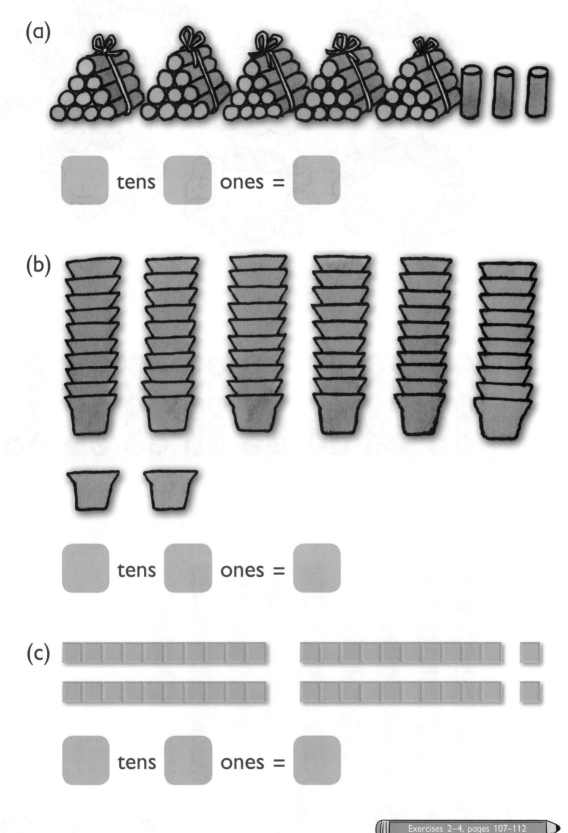

83

4. (a)

70 + 1 =

(b)

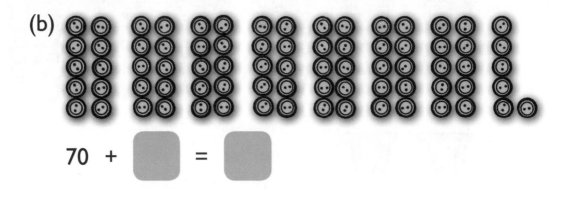

70 + ☐ = ☐

(c)

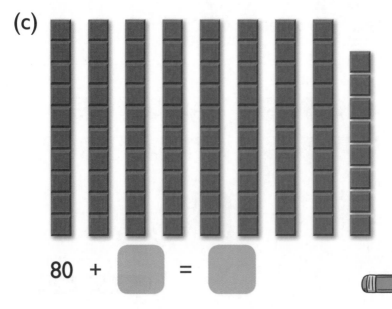

80 + ☐ = ☐

Exercise 5, pages 113–114

10 tens 0 ones
1 hundred
one hundred

100

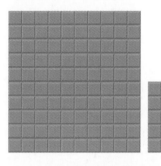

10 tens 5 ones
1 hundred 5 ones
one hundred five

105

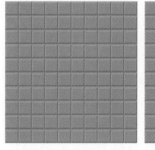

11 tens 0 ones
1 hundred 1 ten
1 hundred 10 ones
one hundred ten

110

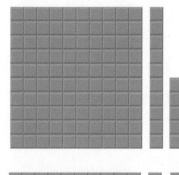

11 tens 5 ones
1 hundred 1 ten 5 ones
1 hundred 15 ones
one hundred fifteen

115

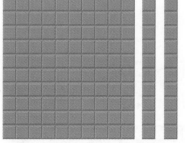

12 tens 0 ones
1 hundred 2 tens
1 hundred 20 ones
one hundred twenty

120

1. Count.

(a)

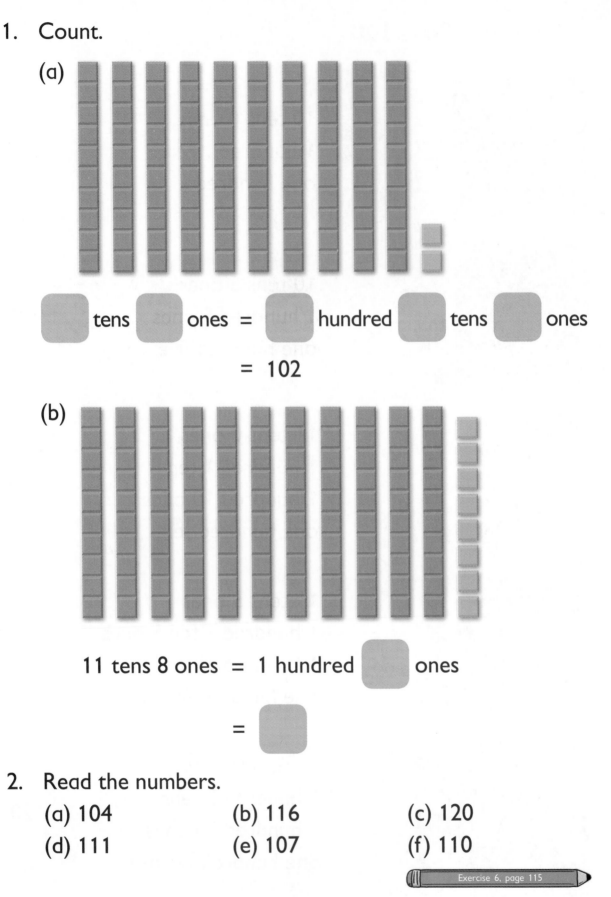

☐ tens ☐ ones = ☐ hundred ☐ tens ☐ ones

= 102

(b)

11 tens 8 ones = 1 hundred ☐ ones

= ☐

2. Read the numbers.

(a) 104   (b) 116   (c) 120
(d) 111   (e) 107   (f) 110

Exercise 6, page 115

3 Estimation

1. Diego has 3 similar jars.
   There are about 10 marbles in Jar A.

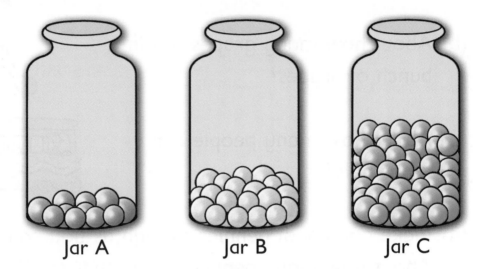

Jar A   Jar B   Jar C

(a) About how many marbles are there in Jar B?

There are about ⬜ marbles in Jar B.

(b) About how many marbles are there in Jar C?

There are about ⬜ marbles in Jar C.

(c) Diego tries to put the marbles from Jars A, B, and C into his pockets.

About how many marbles do you think Diego has in his pockets?

There are about ⬜ marbles altogether in Diego's pockets.

2. Estimate.

(a) About how many marbles can you hold in your hands?

(b) About how many grapes are in a bunch of grapes?

(c) About how many people can a bus hold?

(d) Make a stack of pennies as high as you can. About how many pennies are in the stack? Count them to find the exact number.

3.

Estimate, and then count.

(a) There are about ⬜ people at the beach.

(b) There are exactly ⬜ people at the beach.

Exercise 7, page 116

4 Order of Numbers

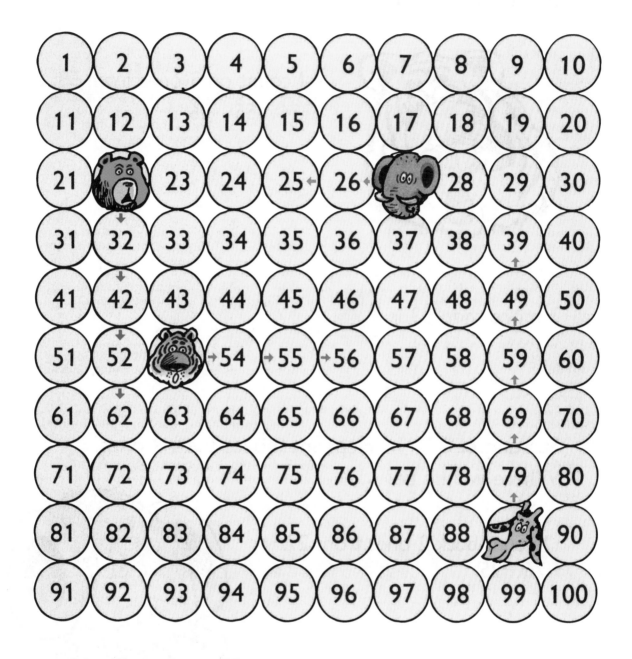

Mr. Tiger is at 53.

Where are Mr. Elephant, Mrs. Bear, and Miss Giraffe?

Starting at 53, Mr. Tiger moves on 3 ones.
Where will he be?

I count on 3 ones from 53:
(54), (55), (56)

3 more than 53 is ⬜ .

Starting at 27, Mr. Elephant moves back 2 ones.
Where will he be?

I count back 2 ones from 27:
(26), (25)

2 less than 27 is ⬜ .

Starting at 22, Mrs. Bear moves on 4 tens.
Where will she be?

I count on 4 tens from 22:
32, 42, 52, 62

40 more than 22 is ___.

Starting at 89, Miss Giraffe moves back 5 tens.
Where will she be?

I count back 5 tens from 89:
79, 69, 59, 49, 39

50 less than 89 is ___.

1.

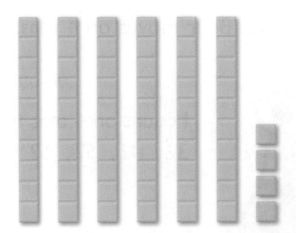

(a) What number is 1 more than 64?

(b) What number is 1 less than 64?

(c) What number is 10 more than 64?

(d) What number is 10 less than 64?

2. The numbers below count on or back in a regular pattern.

    What are the missing numbers? Explain your answers.

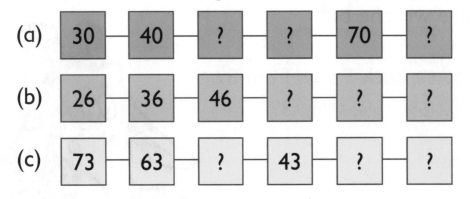

(a) 30 — 40 — ? — ? — 70 — ?

(b) 26 — 36 — 46 — ? — ? — ?

(c) 73 — 63 — ? — 43 — ? — ?

3. (a) What number is 10 more than 52?

    (b) What number is 20 more than 52?

    (c) What number is 10 less than 96?

    (d) What number is 20 less than 96?

Exercises 8–12, pages 117–123

5 Comparing Numbers

I always take the greater amount.

2 tens is greater than 1 ten.

21 is greater than 12.

We write: 21 > 12

Tens	Ones
2	1
1	2

0 ones is less than 9 ones.

90 is less than 99.

We write: 90 < 99

Tens	Ones
9	0
9	9

This sign means **greater than**.

This sign means **less than**.

1. Which sign should you use, **>** or **<**?

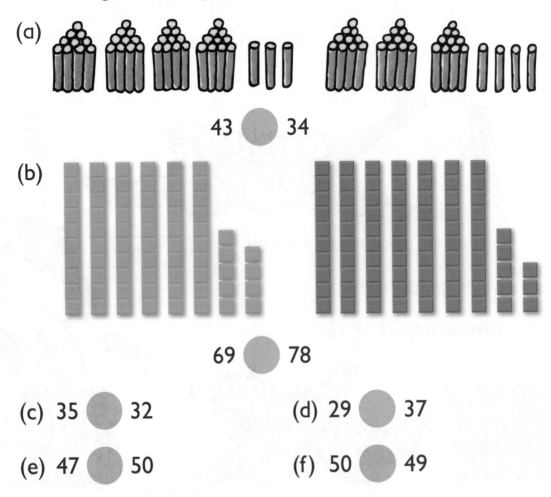

(a)

43 ◯ 34

(b)

69 ◯ 78

(c) 35 ◯ 32   (d) 29 ◯ 37

(e) 47 ◯ 50   (f) 50 ◯ 49

2. (a) Which number is smaller, 40 or 39?

    (b) Which number is greater, 29 or 30?

    (c) Which number is the smallest, 65, 64, or 56?

    (d) Which number is the greatest, 89, 90, or 98?

3. Arrange the numbers in order. Begin with the smallest.

59   95   90   50

Exercise 13, pages 124–127

6 Addition Within 100

Add 54 and 3.

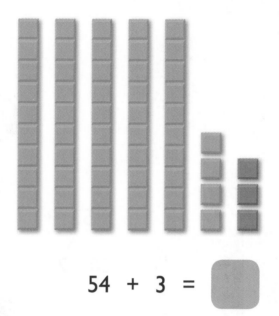

54 + 3 = [ ]

Count on 3 ones from 54:
(55), (56), (57)

54 + 3
50   4
Add 4 and 3.

1. Complete the equations.

(a)

$$65 + 2 = \boxed{}$$

65 + 2
60 5
5 + 2 = ?

(b)

$$52 + 7 = \boxed{}$$

52 + 7
50   2

(c)

$$3 + 46 = \boxed{}$$

46 + 3
40   6

Exercise 14, pages 128–129

2. Complete the equations.

(a)

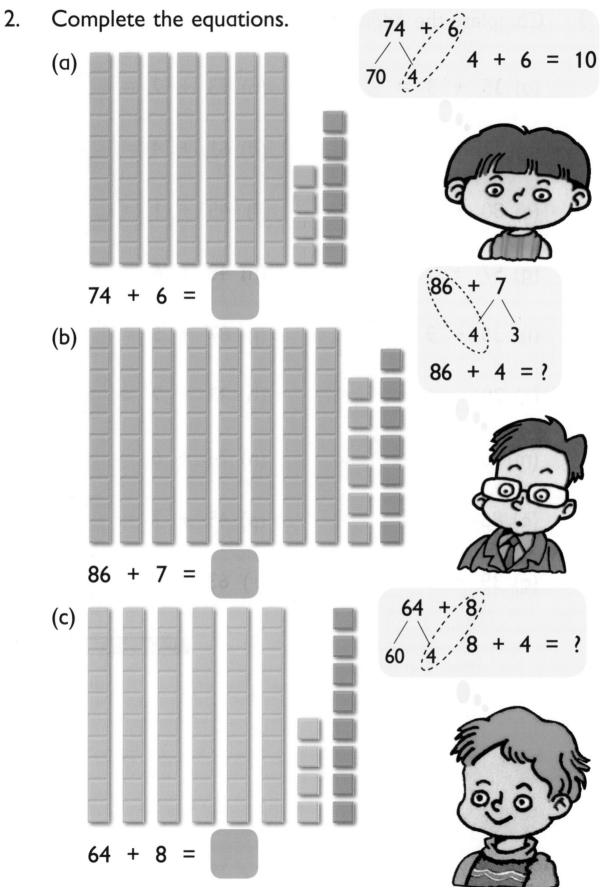

74 + 6 =

$$74 + 6$$
$$70 \quad 4$$
$$4 + 6 = 10$$

(b)

86 + 7 =

$$86 + 7$$
$$4 \quad 3$$
$$86 + 4 = ?$$

(c)

64 + 8 =

$$64 + 8$$
$$60 \quad 4 \quad 8 + 4 = ?$$

3. Complete the addition equations.

(a) 35 + 3 =

(b) 93 + 2 =

(c) 22 + 5 =

(d) 61 + 4 =

(e) 80 + 9 =

(f) 45 + 1 =

(g) 57 + 3 =

(h) 48 + 6 =

(i) 36 + 9 =

(j) 87 + 5 =

(k) 29 + 6 =

(l) 33 + 7 =

(m) 55 + 5 =

(n) 74 + 6 =

(o) 86 + 8 =

(p) 45 + 7 =

(q) 39 + 9 =

(r) 63 + 8 =

Exercise 15, pages 130–132

4. Add 62 and 30.

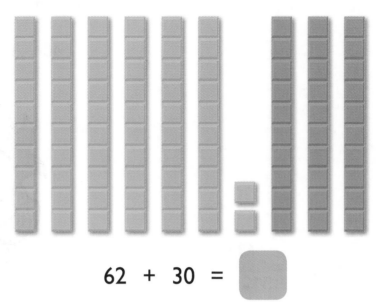

62 + 30 = [ ]

Count on 3 tens from 62:
(72), (82), (92)

62 + 30
/ \
60   2

Add 60 and 30.

Tens	Ones
6	2
+ 3	0

99

5. Complete the equations.

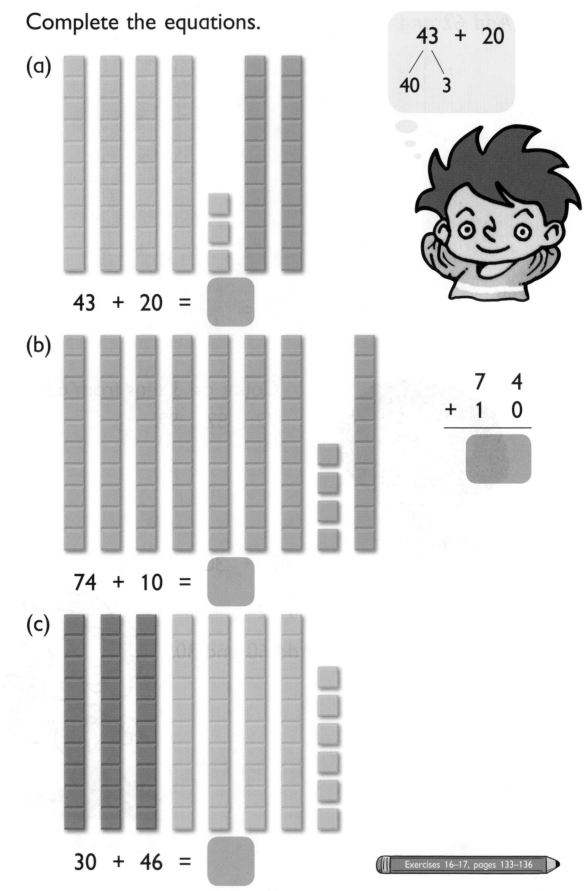

(a)

$43 + 20 =$

$$\begin{array}{r} 4\ 3 \\ + 2\ 0 \\ \hline \end{array}$$

(thought bubble)

43 + 20

40   3

(b)

$74 + 10 =$

$$\begin{array}{r} 7\ 4 \\ + 1\ 0 \\ \hline \end{array}$$

(c)

$30 + 46 =$

Exercises 16–17, pages 133–136

6. Add 32 and 16.

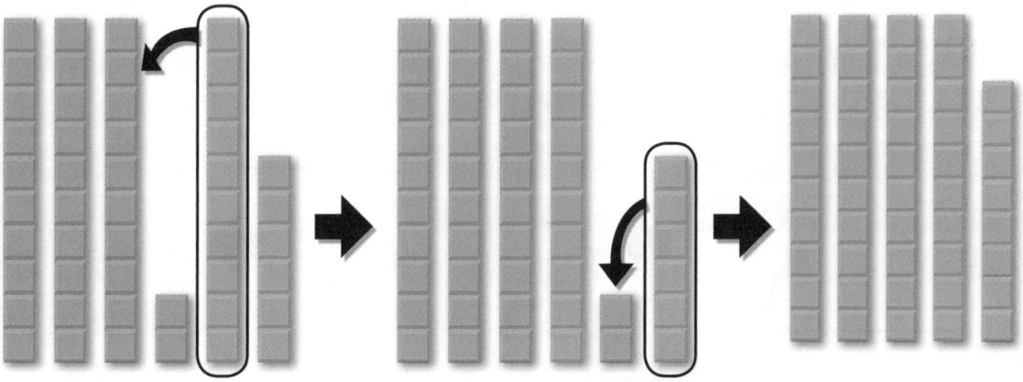

$$32 + 16 = \boxed{}$$

$$32 + 10 + 6$$

7. Add 43 and 35.

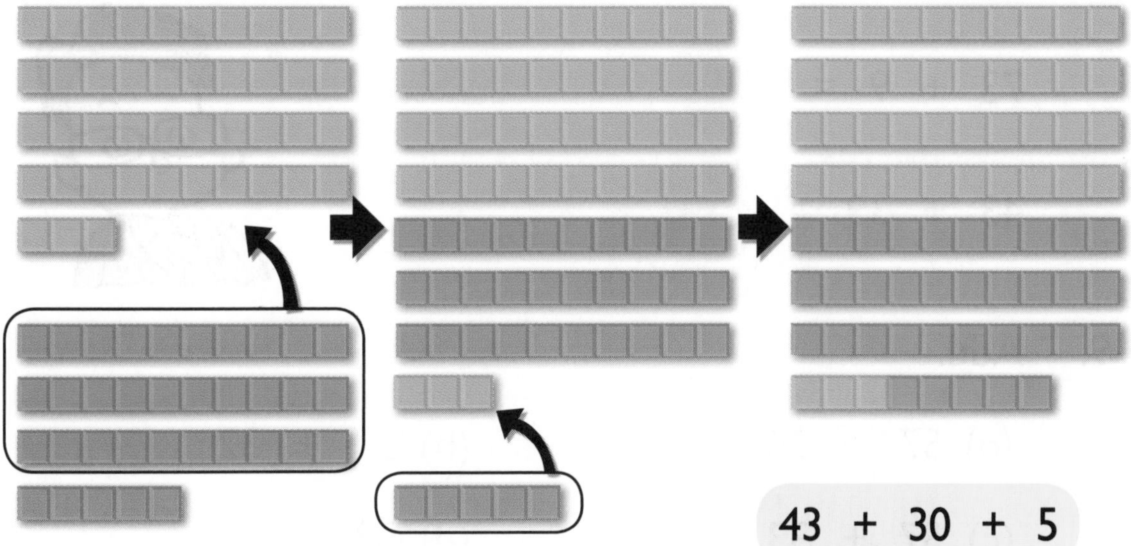

$$43 + 35 = \boxed{}$$

$$43 + 30 + 5$$

Tens	Ones
4	3
+ 3	5

$\boxed{}$

8. Add 43 and 39.

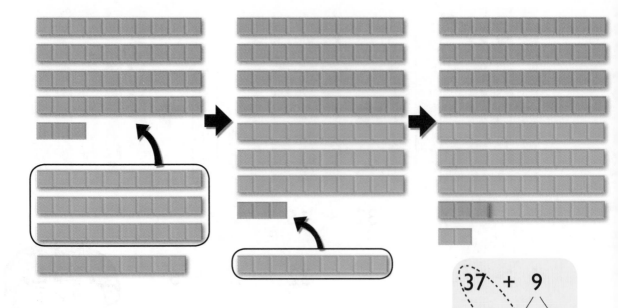

43 + 30 = 73

73 + 9 =

43 + 39 =

37 + 9
  7   2

9. Add.

(a) 57 + 30

(b) 57 + 32

(c) 57 + 33

(d) 57 + 35

(e) 24 + 60

(f) 24 + 65

(g) 24 + 66

(h) 24 + 68

(i) 20 + 72

(j) 18 + 57

Exercise 18, pages 137–139

7 Subtraction Within 100

Subtract 2 from 48.

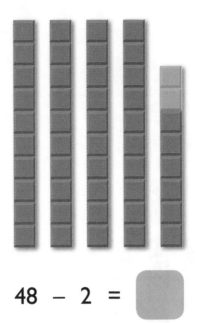

48 − 2 = ☐

Count back 2 ones from 48:
47, 46

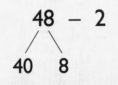

48 − 2

40   8

Subtract 2 from 8.

1. Subtract.

(a)

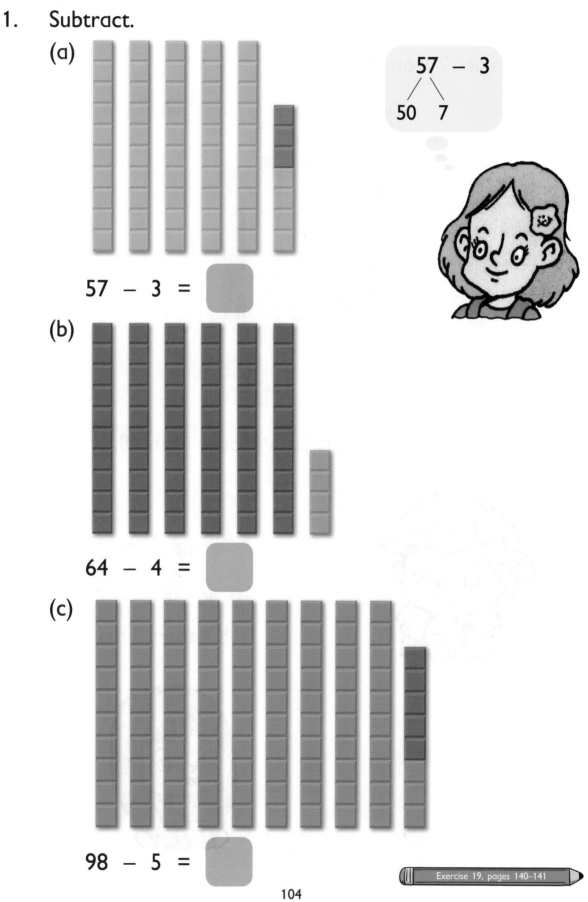

57 − 3

50   7

57 − 3 = ☐

(b)

64 − 4 = ☐

(c)

98 − 5 = ☐

Exercise 19, pages 140–141

2. Subtract.

(a)

$$60 - 3 = \boxed{}$$

60 − 3

50   10

10 − 3 = 7
50 + 7 = ?

(b)

$$50 - 6 = \boxed{}$$

50 − 6

40   10

10 − 6 = 4
40 + 4 = ?

(c)

$$53 - 6 = \boxed{}$$

53 − 6

50   3

50 − 6 = 44
44 + 3 = ?

(d)

$$82 - 7$$
$$12 - 7 = 5$$
$$70 \quad 12 \quad 70 + 5 = ?$$

$$82 - 7 = \boxed{}$$

(e)

$$85 - 9$$
$$85 - 5 = 80$$
$$5 \quad 4 \quad 80 - 4 = ?$$

$$85 - 9 = \boxed{}$$

3. Subtract.

(a) $70 - 6$ (b) $60 - 4$

(c) $65 - 3$ (d) $65 - 5$

(e) $65 - 6$ (f) $65 - 8$

(g) $86 - 3$ (h) $57 - 5$

(i) $92 - 9$ (j) $94 - 8$

Exercise 20, pages 142–144

4. Subtract.

(a)

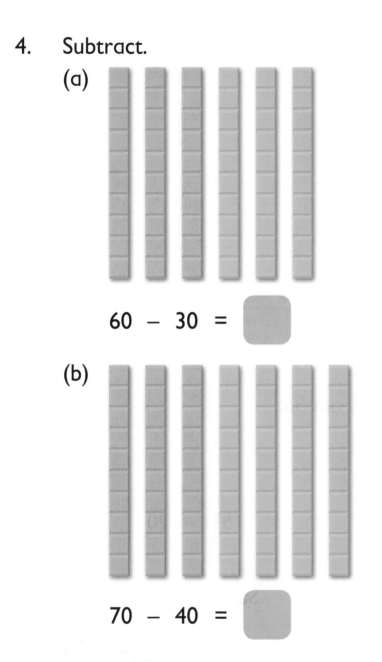

6 tens − 3 tens

60 − 30 = ▢

(b)

70 − 40 = ▢

5. Subtract.

(a) 9 − 5   (b) 90 − 50

(c) 8 − 4   (d) 80 − 40

(e) 60 − 5   (f) 60 − 50

(g) 70 − 50   (h) 80 − 2

6. Subtract 20 from 53.

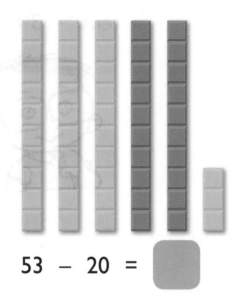

53 − 20 = ◻

Count back 2 tens from 53:
(43), (33)

53 − 20
  ╱   ╲
50   3
Subtract 20 from 50.

Tens	Ones
5	3
− 2	0

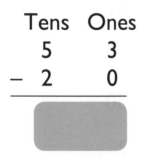

7. Complete the equations.

(a)

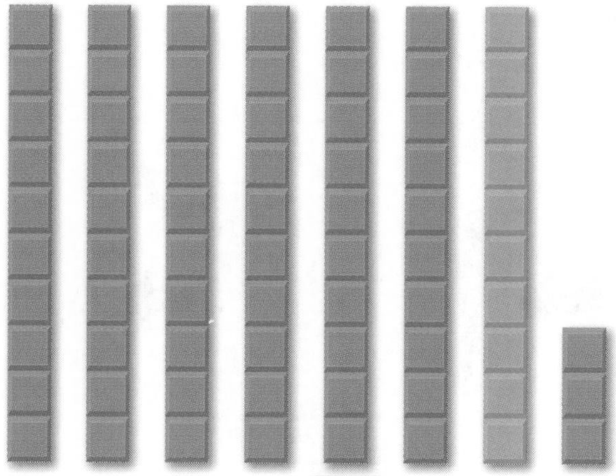

73 − 10 = ▢

73 − 10
70   3

(b)

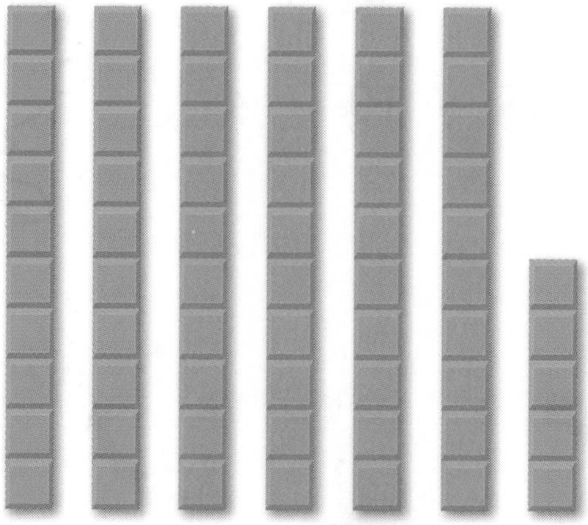

65 − 40 = ▢

$$\begin{array}{r} 6\ 5 \\ -\ 4\ 0 \\ \hline \end{array}$$

▢

(c)

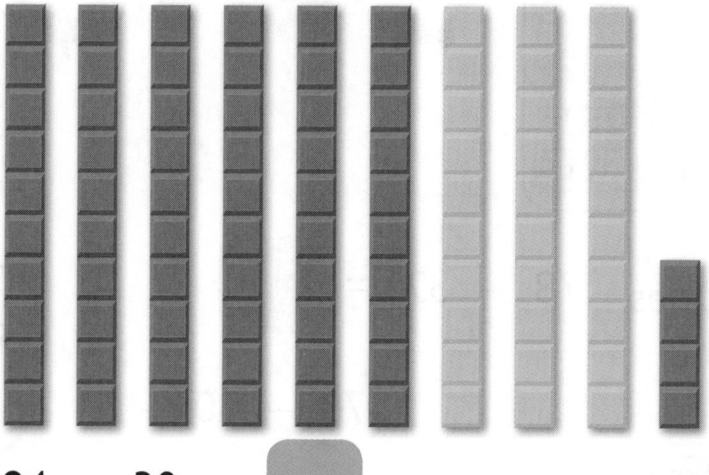

94 − 30 = ▢

Exercises 21–22, pages 145–148

8. Subtract 14 from 56.

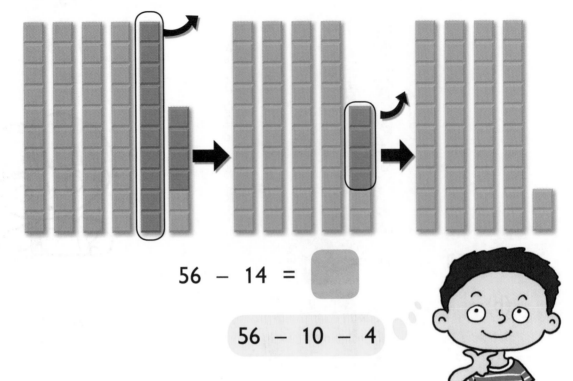

56 − 14 = ⬜

56 − 10 − 4

9. Subtract 32 from 78.

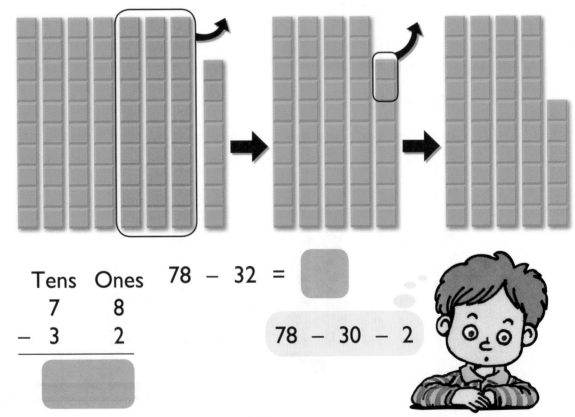

Tens	Ones
7	8
− 3	2

78 − 32 = ⬜

78 − 30 − 2

10. Subtract 36 from 72.

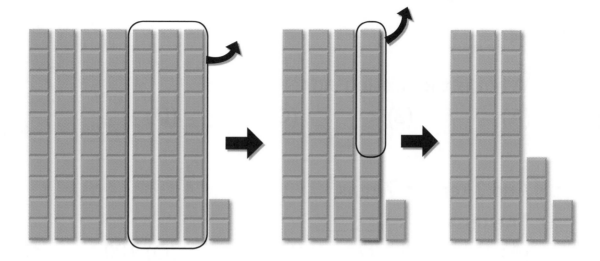

72 − 30 = 42

42 − 6 = ▢

72 − 36 = ▢

72 − 30 − 6

11. Subtract.

(a) 57 − 30

(b) 57 − 32

(c) 57 − 37

(d) 57 − 39

(e) 64 − 30

(f) 64 − 25

(g) 66 − 24

(h) 66 − 28

(i) 70 − 32

(j) 80 − 57

Exercise 23, pages 149–151

1. 54 _____ 56

    What is the missing sign?
    (A) >   (B) <   (C) =   (D) +

2. Add 3 tens to 7 tens.
    The answer is _____.
    (A) 10   (B) 37   (C) 73   (D) 100

3. Select True or False.
    37 + 28 = 57 + 8   True / False

4. Select True or False.
    47 − 13 = 6 tens   True / False

5. Josh collected 65 seashells.
    30 of them were broken.
    He kept only the unbroken seashells.
    How many seashells did he keep?

6. Mira had 58 books.
    She bought another 8 books.
    How many books does she have altogether?

7. Kathy bought some pansies.
    She planted 35 of them and has 25 more to plant.
    How many pansies did she buy?

8. Jill had 82 eggs.
    She used 27 of them for baking.
    How many eggs does Jill have left?

9. Add 34 and 8.
    Show how you add these numbers.
    Explain your answer.

1.

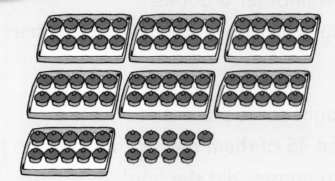

How many cupcakes are there?

(A) 69 ones

(B) 6 tens 9 ones

(C) 7 tens 9 ones

(D) 79 tens

2. 95 is _____ more than 65.

(A) 10

(B) 20

(C) 30

(D) 40

3. Select True or False.
   20 + 7 = 9 + 9 + 9   True / False

4. Select True or False.
   45 − 12 = 63 − 10   True / False

5. Jay has **46** red apples.

   Seth has **7** green apples.

   How many apples do they have altogether?

6. Sara has **89** toy planes.

   She gives **26** of them to her brother.

   How many toy planes does Sara have now?

7. Linda baked **68** cookies in the morning.

   She baked another **10** cookies in the afternoon.

   How many cookies did Linda bake altogether?

8. Kelvin had some walnuts.

   He gave **45** walnuts to his neighbour and **55** walnuts to his friend.

   He had no walnuts left.

   How many walnuts did Kelvin have at first?

9. Peter has **3** envelopes.

   Each envelope contains **10** stamps.

   John has **32** stamps.

   Who has more stamps?

   Explain your answer.

Workbook Review 16, pages 152–154

17 MONEY

1 Bills and Coins

We use these coins and bills in the United States.

Do you know their values?

penny

dime

half-dollar

nickel

quarter

one dollar

five dollars

ten dollars

twenty dollars

The penny has the smallest value of all the coins.

Its value is 1 cent.

The nickel has a value of 5 cents.

The dime has a value of

 cents.

The quarter has a value of

cents.

1.

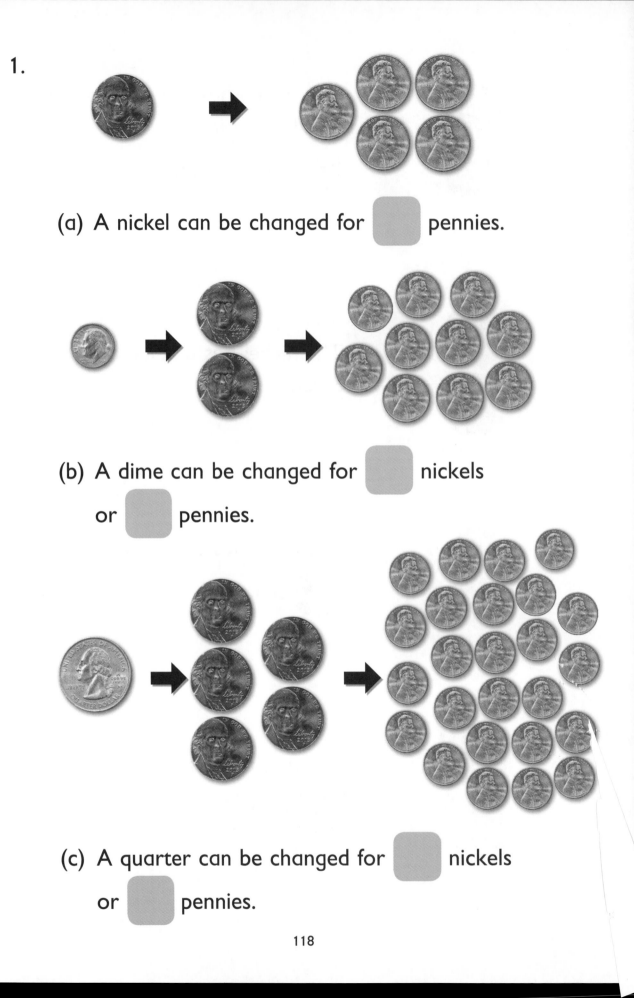

(a) A nickel can be changed for ⬜ pennies.

(b) A dime can be changed for ⬜ nickels

or ⬜ pennies.

(c) A quarter can be changed for ⬜ nickels

or ⬜ pennies.

6. Fill in the blanks.

25, 50,...

(a) 1 quarter = ☐ cents

(b) 2 quarters = ☐ cents

(c) 3 quarters = ☐ cents

(d) 4 quarters = ☐ cents

7. Fill in the blanks.

Mary paid this amount of money for a notebook.

NOTE BOOK

25, 50, 60, 70, 80, 90, 95 cents

The notebook cost ☐ ¢.

8. 1 quarter + 1 nickel = 30 cents

25, 30, 40, 50, 55, 56, 57 cents

The total amount of money = ☐ ¢

121

9. How much money is there in each set of coins?

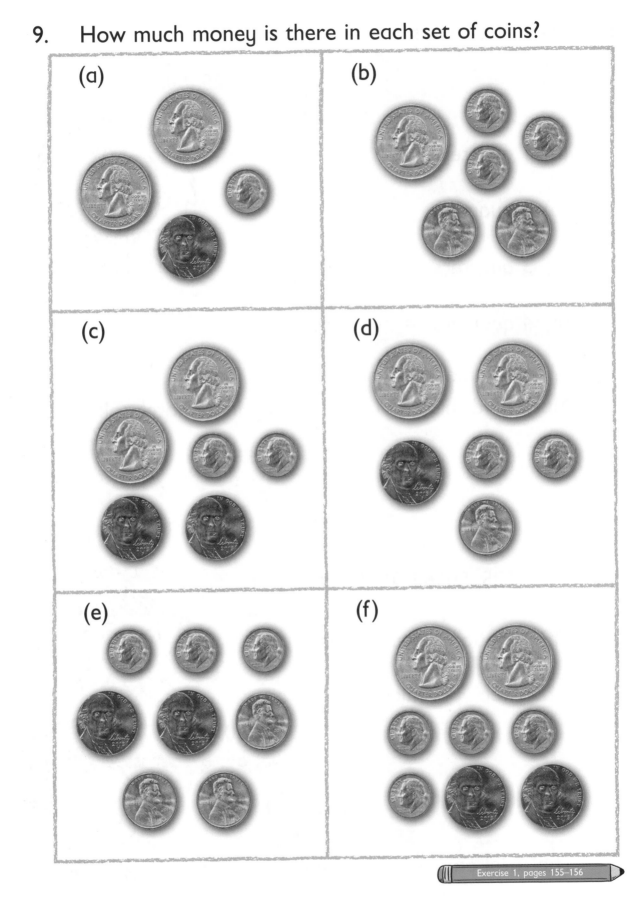

(a)

(b)

(c)

(d)

(e)

(f)

Exercise 1, pages 155–156

10. Fill in the blanks.

(a)

A ten-dollar bill can be changed for

[ ] five-dollar bills.

(b) What other bills can a ten-dollar bill be changed for?

(c) What bills can a twenty-dollar bill be changed for?

11. Fill in the blanks.
Maria paid this amount of money for a doll.

10, 15, 16, 17 dollars

The doll cost $[ ].

12. How much money is there in each set?

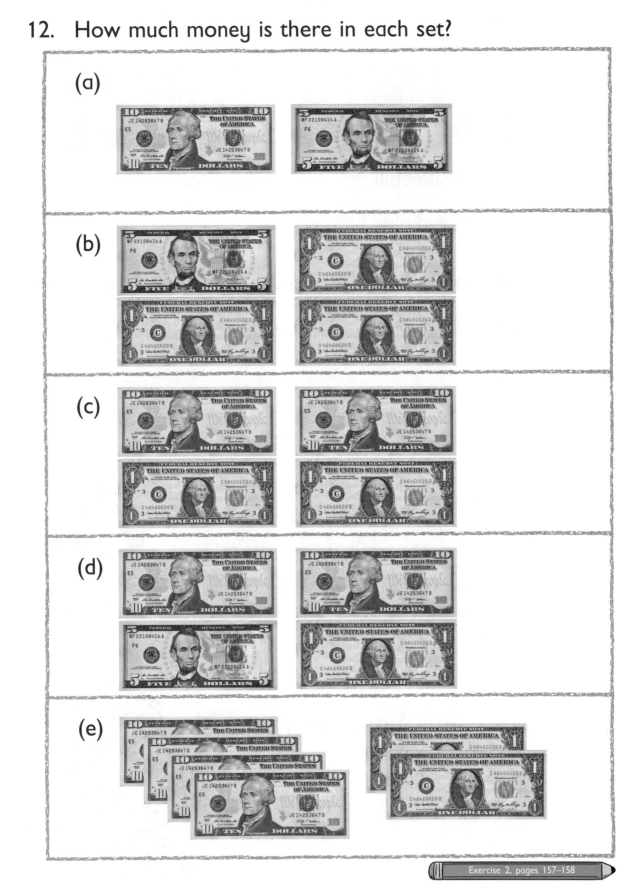

(a)

(b)

(c)

(d)

(e)

Exercise 2, pages 157–158

13. Which set has a greater amount of money?

(a)

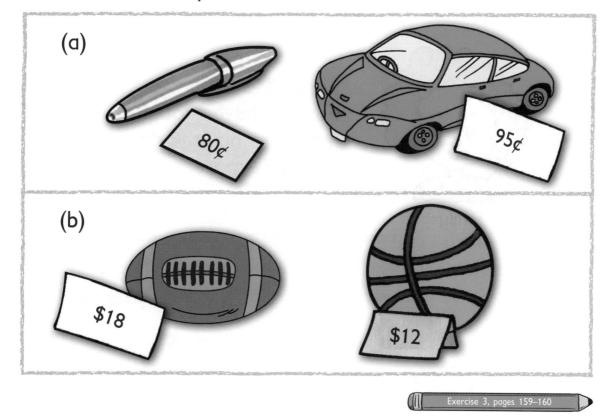

Set A   Set B

(b)

Set X   Set Y

14. Which is cheaper?

(a)

80¢   95¢

(b)

$18 $12

Exercise 3, pages 159–160

2 Shopping

$17

I have $20.
I have $3 left after buying the doll.

$20 − $17 = $3

Dani

I have $15.
I do not have enough money to buy the doll.
I need $2 more.

Emily

$17 − $15 = $2

126

Write the missing number.

1.

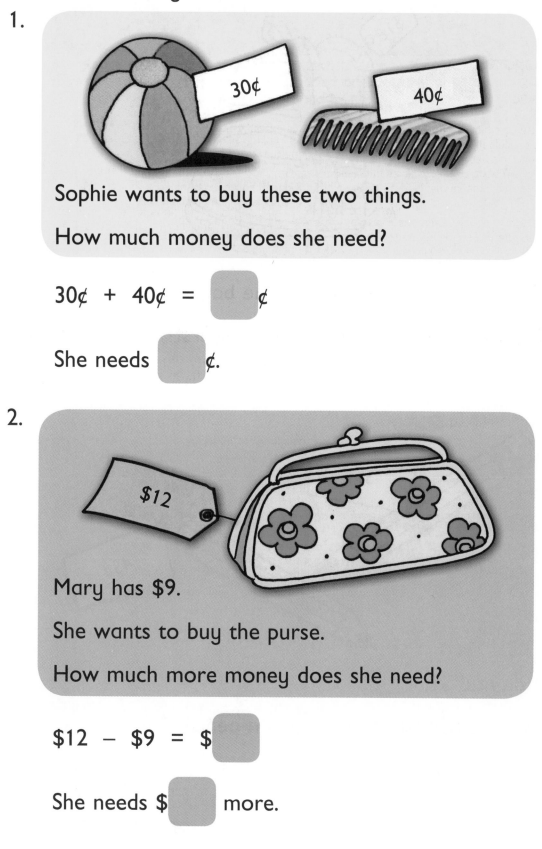

Sophie wants to buy these two things.

How much money does she need?

30¢ + 40¢ = [ ] ¢

She needs [ ] ¢.

2.

Mary has $9.

She wants to buy the purse.

How much more money does she need?

$12 − $9 = $ [ ]

She needs $ [ ] more.

3.

Ali had $2 left after buying the bag.

How much money did he have at first?

4.

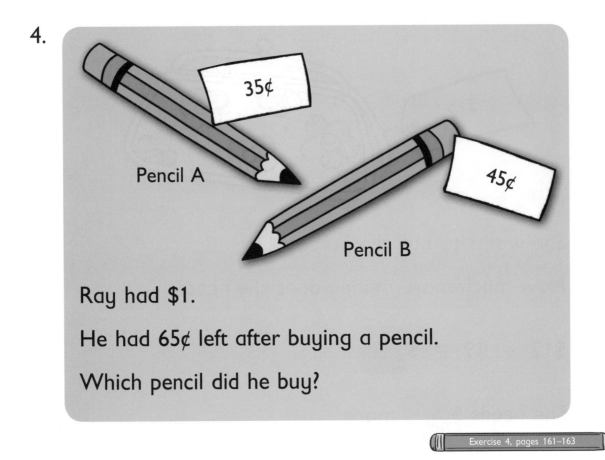

Pencil A

Pencil B

Ray had $1.

He had 65¢ left after buying a pencil.

Which pencil did he buy?

Exercise 4, pages 161–163

1. David has **8** nickels.

    He has _____ cents.

    (A) 8   (B) 20   (C) 40   (D) 50

2.

    The book costs $ _____.

    (A) 16   (B) 21   (C) 25   (D) 30

3. Select True or False.

    The three items cost $15 altogether.   True / False

4. Select True or False.

    Simon had $12.

    He bought a pair of shoes and had $2 left.

    The pair of shoes cost $8.   True / False

5.

Set A   Set B

(a) How much money is there in Set A?

(b) How much money is there in Set B?

(c) Which set has more money?

(d) How much more?
     Write a subtraction equation.

6. Iris bought this present for her mother.
   She had $18 left.
   How much money did she have at first?

   $39

7. Caryn has $42.
   Miguel has $84.
   How much more money does Miguel have than Caryn?

8.

Sally has $23.
Can she buy all of these items? Explain your answer.

Workbook Review 17, pages 164–174

Word	Meaning
divide	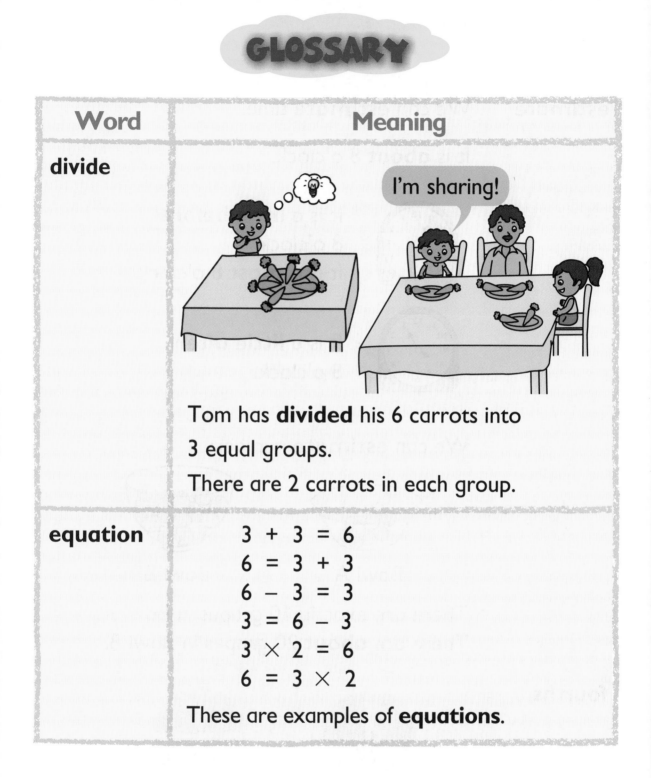 I'm sharing! Tom has **divided** his 6 carrots into 3 equal groups. There are 2 carrots in each group.
equation	3 + 3 = 6 6 = 3 + 3 6 − 3 = 3 3 = 6 − 3 3 × 2 = 6 6 = 3 × 2 These are examples of **equations**.

Word	Meaning
estimate	We can **estimate** time.

We can **estimate** time.

It is **about** 8 o'clock.

 It is a **little before**
8 o'clock.
It is **almost** 8 o'clock.

 It is a **little after**
8 o'clock.

We can **estimate** numbers.

Bowl A   Bowl B

There are exactly 10 grapes in Bowl A.
There are **about** 20 grapes in Bowl B.

fourths

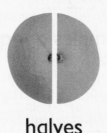 

halves   **fourths**

When we cut 1 whole into 4 equal parts,
we have 4 **fourths**.

Word	Meaning
greater than	82 is 2 more than 80. 82 is **greater than** 80. 82 > 80 We write **>** to mean **greater than**.
group	We put things in equal groups when we multiply or divide. 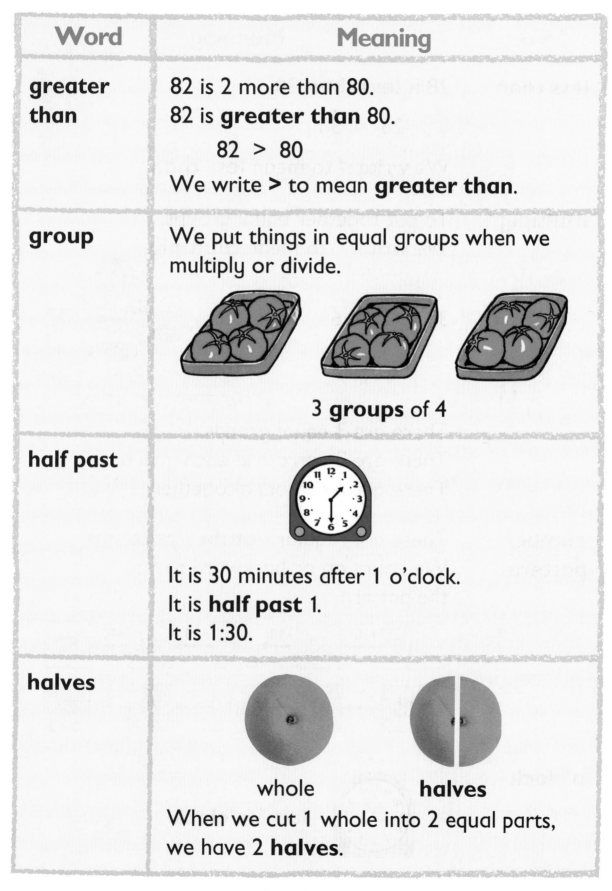 <div align="center">3 **groups** of 4</div>
half past	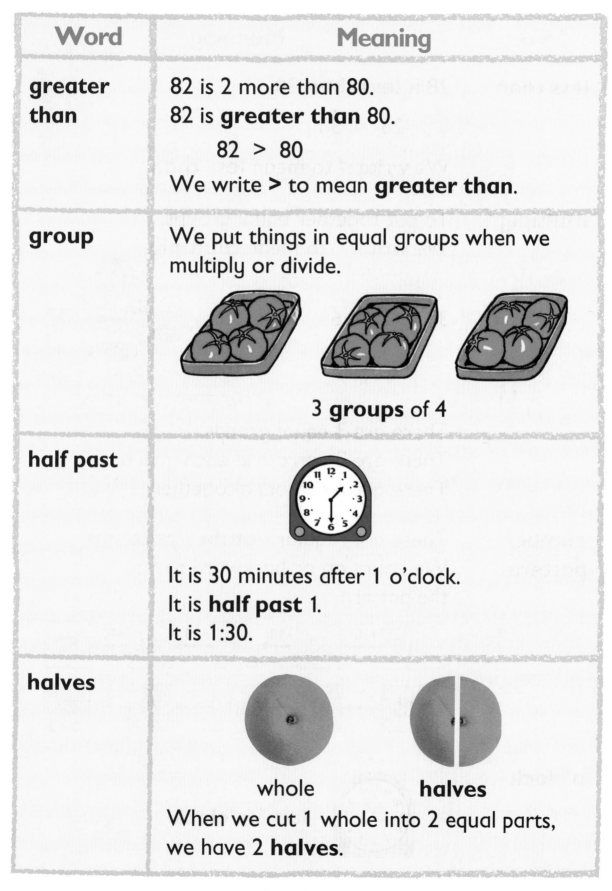 It is 30 minutes after 1 o'clock. It is **half past** 1. It is 1:30.
halves	whole **halves** When we cut 1 whole into 2 equal parts, we have 2 **halves**.

Word	Meaning
less than	28 is **less than** 30. 28 < 30 We write **<** to mean **less than**.
multiply	To put together equal groups. We write × to mean **multiply**. 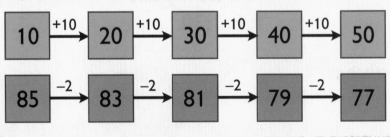 3 × 2 = 6 There are 3 equal groups. There are 2 carrots in each group. There are 6 carrots altogether.
number pattern	These are regular **number patterns**. We count on or backward to find the pattern. 10 →+10 20 →+10 30 →+10 40 →+10 50 85 →−2 83 →−2 81 →−2 79 →−2 77
o'clock	 It is 1 **o'clock**.

Word	Meaning
ones	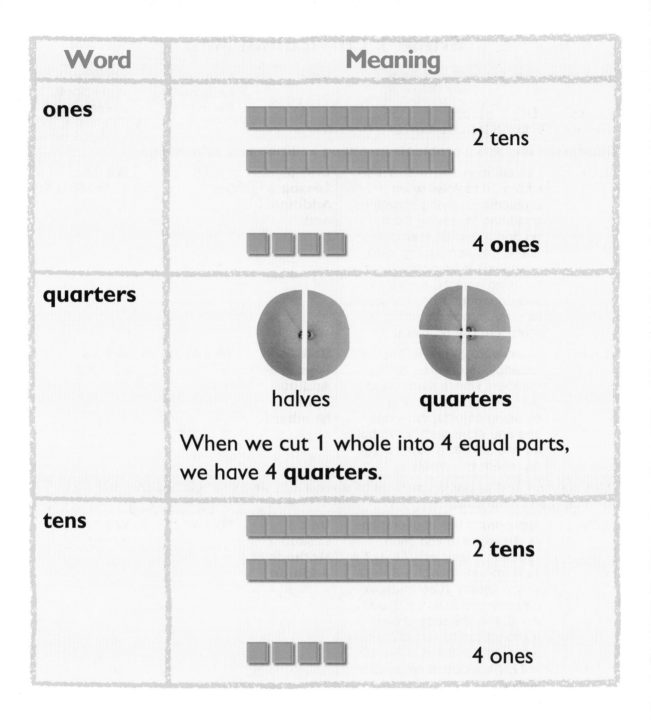 2 tens 4 **ones**
quarters	halves · **quarters** When we cut 1 whole into 4 equal parts, we have 4 **quarters**.
tens	2 **tens** 4 ones

Grade 1 Curriculum Map

Common Core State Standards		Unit	Student Textbook Pages	Student Workbook Exercises
OPERATIONS AND ALGEBRAIC THINKING				
Represent and solve problems involving addition and subtraction.				
1.OA.1	Use addition and subtraction within 20 to solve word problems involving situations of adding to, taking from, putting together, taking apart, and comparing, with unknowns in all positions, e.g., by using objects, drawings, and equations with a symbol for the unknown number to represent the problem.	**Unit 6 Lesson 2 Addition and Subtraction**	**TB 1A:** 89, 94	**WB 1A:** 127–129, 133
1.OA.2	Solve word problems that call for addition of three whole numbers whose sum is less than or equal to 20, e.g., by using objects, drawings, and equations with a symbol for the unknown number to represent the problem.	**Unit 11 Lesson 5 Adding Three Numbers**	**TB 1B:** 33–35	**WB 1B:** 43–47
Understand and apply properties of operations and the relationship between addition and subtraction.				
1.OA.3	Apply properties of operations as strategies to add and subtract. *Examples: If 8 + 3 = 11 is known, then 3 + 8 = 11 is also known. (Commutative property of addition.) To add 2 + 6 + 4, the second two numbers can be added to make a ten, so 2 + 6 + 4 = 2 + 10 = 12. (Associative property of addition.)*	**Unit 3 Lesson 2 Methods of Addition**	**TB 1A:** 37	**WB 1A:** 37–39
1.OA.4	Understand subtraction as an unknown-addend problem. *For example, subtract 10 – 8 by finding the number that makes 10 when added to 8.*	**Unit 4 Lesson 2 Methods of Subtraction**	**TB 1A:** 56–58, 60	**WB 1A:** 60–63, 66–68

Common Core State Standards		Unit	Student Textbook Pages	Student Workbook Exercises
Add and subtract within 20.				
1.OA.5	Relate counting to addition and subtraction (e.g., by counting on 2 to add 2).	**Unit 3 Lesson 2 Methods of Addition** **Unit 4 Lesson 2 Methods of Subtraction** **Unit 6 Lesson 2 Addition and Subtraction**	**TB 1A:** 40–42, 61–62, 88	**WB 1A:** 42–45, 69–70, 122–126
1.OA.6	Add and subtract within 20, demonstrating fluency for addition and subtraction within 10. Use strategies such as counting on; making ten (e.g., $8 + 6 = 8 + 2 + 4 = 10 + 4 = 14$); decomposing a number leading to a ten (e.g., $13 - 4 = 13 - 3 - 1 = 10 - 1 = 9$); using the relationship between addition and subtraction (e.g., knowing that $8 + 4 = 12$, one knows $12 - 8 = 4$); and creating equivalent but easier or known sums (e.g., adding $6 + 7$ by creating the known equivalent $6 + 6 + 1 = 12 + 1 = 13$).	**Unit 6 Lesson 2 Addition and Subtraction** **Unit 11 Lesson 4 Addition and Subtraction**	**TB 1A:** 82–87 **TB 1B:** 28–31	**WB 1A:** 107–121 **WB 1B:** 32–39
Work with addition and subtraction equations.				
1.OA.7	Understand the meaning of the equal sign, and determine if equations involving addition and subtraction are true or false. *For example, which of the following equations are true and which are false? $6 = 6$, $7 = 8 - 1$, $5 + 2 = 2 + 5$, $4 + 1 = 5 + 2$.*	**Unit 3 Lesson 2 Methods of Addition** **Unit 4 Lesson 2 Methods of Subtraction**	**TB 1A:** 32, 46, 66	**WB 1A:** 48–49, 76–81
1.OA.8	Determine the unknown whole number in an addition or subtraction equation relating three whole numbers. *For example, determine the unknown number that makes the equation true in each of the equations $8 + ? = 11$, $5 = \square - 3$, $6 + 6 = \square$.*	**Unit 6 Lesson 2 Addition and Subtraction**	**TB 1A:** 89, 92–93	**WB 1A:** 127–129, 130–132

Common Core State Standards		Unit	Student Textbook Pages	Student Workbook Exercises
NUMBER AND OPERATIONS IN BASE TEN				
Extend the counting sequence.				
1.NBT.1	Count to 120, starting at any number less than 120. In this range, read and write numerals and represent a number of objects with a written numeral.	**Unit 1 Lesson 1 Counting** **Unit 6 Lesson 1 Counting and Comparing** **Unit 11 Lesson 1 Counting** **Unit 16 Lesson 1 Tens and Ones** **Unit 16 Lesson 2 Count Past 100** **Unit 16 Lesson 4 Order of Numbers**	**TB 1A:** 8–13, 74–75 **TB 1B:** 8–12, 14, 78–83, 85–86, 89-92	**WB 1A:** 8–11 **WB 1B:** 7–10, 11, 14-15, 104–106, 107–112, 115, 118-120, 121-123
Understand place value.				
1.NBT.2a	Understand that the two digits of a two-digit number represent amounts of tens and ones. Understand the following as special cases: 10 can be thought of as a bundle of ten ones — called a "ten."	**Unit 11 Lesson 2 Tens and Ones** **Unit 16 Lesson 1 Tens and Ones**	**TB 1B:** 12-13, 15–17, 78–83	**WB 1B:** 11-13, 16–17, 104–105, 107, 109–110
1.NBT.2b	Understand that the two digits of a two-digit number represent amounts of tens and ones. Understand the following as special cases: The numbers from 11 to 19 are composed of a ten and one, two, three, four, five, six, seven, eight, or nine ones.	**Unit 6 Lesson 1 Counting and Comparing**	**TB 1A:** 75–78	**WB 1A:** 95–99, 100–101

Common Core State Standards		Unit	Student Textbook Pages	Student Workbook Exercises
1.NBT.2c	Understand that the two digits of a two-digit number represent amounts of tens and ones. Understand the following as special cases: The numbers 10, 20, 30, 40, 50, 60, 70, 80, 90 refer to one, two, three, four, five, six, seven, eight, or nine tens (and 0 ones).	**Unit 16 Lesson 1 Tens and Ones**	**TB 1B:** 78–81	**WB 1B:** 104–106
1.NBT.3	Compare two two-digit numbers based on meanings of the tens and ones digits, recording the results of comparisons with the symbols >, =, and <.	**Unit 16 Lesson 4 Order of Numbers** **Unit 16 Lesson 5 Comparing Numbers**	**TB 1B:** 93–94	**WB 1B:** 117, 124–127
Use place value understanding and properties of operations to add and subtract.				
1.NBT.4	Add within 100, including adding a two-digit number and a one-digit number, and adding a two-digit number and a multiple of 10, using concrete models or drawings and strategies based on place value, properties of operations, and/or the relationship between addition and subtraction; relate the strategy to a written method and explain the reasoning used. Understand that in adding two-digit numbers, one adds tens and tens, ones and ones; and sometimes it is necessary to compose a ten.	**Unit 16 Lesson 4 Order of Numbers** **Unit 16 Lesson 6 Addition Within 100**	**TB 1B:** 24, 25, 26-27, 28, 95–102	**WB 1B:** 24-25, 26-27, 28-31, 32-34, 128–139
1.NBT.5	Given a two-digit number, mentally find 10 more or 10 less than the number, without having to count; explain the reasoning used.	**Unit 11 Lesson 2 Tens and Ones** **Unit 11 Lesson 4 Addition and Subtraction**	**TB 1B:** 18–19, 24	**WB 1B:** 18–20, 24-25

Common Core State Standards		Unit	Student Textbook Pages	Student Workbook Exercises
1.NBT.6	Subtract multiples of 10 in the range 10–90 from multiples of 10 in the range 10–90 (positive or zero differences), using concrete models or drawings and strategies based on place value, properties of operations, and/or the relationship between addition and subtraction; relate the strategy to a written method and explain the reasoning used.	**Unit 11 Lesson 4 Addition and Subtraction** **Unit 16 Lesson 7 Subtraction Within 100**	**TB 1B:** 24, 107–109	**WB 1B:** 24-25, 145–148
MEASUREMENT AND DATA				
Measure lengths indirectly and by iterating length units.				
1.MD.1	Order three objects by length; compare the lengths of two objects indirectly by using a third object.	**Unit 8 Lesson 1 Comparing Length**	**TB 1A:** 115–119	**WB 1A:** 165–169
1.MD.2	Express the length of an object as a whole number of length units, by laying multiple copies of a shorter object (the length unit) end to end; understand that the length measurement of an object is the number of same-size length units that span it with no gaps or overlaps. *Limit to contexts where the object being measured is spanned by a whole number of length units with no gaps or overlaps.*	**Unit 8 Lesson 2 Measuring Length**	**TB 1A:** 120–121	**WB 1A:** 170–172
Tell and write time.				
1.MD.3	Tell and write time in hours and half-hours using analog and digital clocks.	**Unit 15 Lesson 1 Telling Time**	**TB 1B:** 68–71	**WB 1B:** 91–96

Common Core State Standards		Unit	Student Textbook Pages	Student Workbook Exercises
Represent and interpret data.				
1.MD.4	Organize, represent, and interpret data with up to three categories; ask and answer questions about the total number of data points, how many in each category, and how many more or less are in one category than in another.	**Unit 10 Lesson 1 Graphs**	**TB 1A:** 134–139	**WB 1A:** 195–205
GEOMETRY				
Reason with shapes and their attributes.				
1.G.1	Distinguish between defining attributes (e.g., triangles are closed and three-sided) versus non-defining attributes (e.g., color, orientation, overall size); build and draw shapes to possess defining attributes.	**Unit 7 Lesson 1 Common Shapes**	**TB 1A:** 100–106, 109–110	**WB 1A:** 144–154
1.G.2	Compose two-dimensional shapes (rectangles, squares, trapezoids, triangles, half-circles, and quarter-circles) or three-dimensional shapes (cubes, right rectangular prisms, right circular cones, and right circular cylinders) to create a composite shape, and compose new shapes from the composite shape.	**Unit 7 Lesson 1 Common Shapes**	**TB 1A:** 109–112	**WB 1A:** 159–160
1.G.3	Partition circles and rectangles into two and four equal shares, describe the shares using the words *halves, fourths*, and *quarters*, and use the phrases *half of, fourth of*, and *quarter of*. Describe the whole as two of, or four of the shares. Understand for these examples that decomposing into more equal shares creates smaller shares.	**Unit 14 Lesson 1 Making Halves and Fourths**	**TB 1B:** 65	**WB 1B:** 84–87

Index